YOUR KNOWLEDGE H

Bibliographic information published by the German National Library:

The German National Library lists this publication in the National Bibliography; detailed bibliographic data are available on the Internet at http://dnb.dnb.de .

Imprint:

Copyright © 2019 GRIN Verlag
Print and binding: Books on Demand GmbH, Norderstedt Germany
ISBN: 9783668895232

This book at GRIN:

https://www.grin.com/document/456165

Yakob Tilahun

Organizational Identification, Job Involvement, Percived Organizational Justice as Predictors of Organizational Citizenship Behavior in the Secretariat of Ethiopia's Parliament

GRIN Verlag

GRIN - Your knowledge has value

Since its foundation in 1998, GRIN has specialized in publishing academic texts by students, college teachers and other academics as e-book and printed book. The website www.grin.com is an ideal platform for presenting term papers, final papers, scientific essays, dissertations and specialist books.

Addis Ababa University

College of Education and Behavioral Studies

School of Psychology

Organizational Identification, Job Involvement, Perceived Organizational Justice as Predictors of Organizational Citizenship Behavior in the Secretariat of Ethiopia's Parliament

By: Yakob Tilahun

A Thesis Submitted to the School of Psychology of Addis Ababa University in Partial Fulfillment of the Requirements for the Master of Arts Degree in Social Psychology

October, 2018
Addis Ababa, Ethiopia

Acknowledgements

This paper is completed with the support of different peoples and organizations. Especially my Advisor Tamirie Andualem (PhD) has been keen to keep an eye on me with all his Knowledge and expertise, for that, I would like to express my sincere gratefulness for what he has done for the completion of the research. It is also a great honor indeed to be his advisee.

The process of the research has also been shaped with the help of the organization in the study area. For this to happen, Secretariat of the House of Peoples Representatives of FDRE and its staff members have been playing a pivotal role, and I strongly appreciate their support and cordiality.

Regarding the data collection process, I have been assisted by two preeminent people, Ato Netsanet Amsalu and Ato Gezehage Ketema, because they have the experience of facilitating such works. For the pilot test purpose, I have also been helped by two staff members from the Secretariat of the House of Federation, namely Laqachew Demel and Amaha Neway. I wish them all the best in their professional endeavors with thanks.

Furthermore, I would like to show express my appreciation to W/O Teshay Tekle for her endorsed facilitation of financial resources and to all my office colleagues, especially Ato Asmare Kassahun, Ato Wudetaw Libase, Ato Kasssaye Arega, W/O Alemnesh Nigussie, Ato Yared Eshetu and Ato Yakob Woldesemayiat for their versatile support and participation of examining some technical aspects of the research scales.

Finally, as always, my family members backed me to successfully finish this program with their prayer and care. It is a great privilege to have you all the time. In sum, all that was not be possible without God's will.

Table of Contents

Chapter Three

Methods..36

List of Tables and Figures   Page

List of Abbreviations & Acronyms

FDRE   Federal Democratic Republic of Ethiopia

SHOPR   Secretariat of the House of Peoples Representatives

OID   Organizational Identification

JI   Job Involvement

OJ   Organizational Justice

DJ   Distributive Justice

PJ   Procedural Justice

IJ   Interactional Justice

OCB   Organizational Citizenship Behavior

OCB- I   Organizational Citizenship Behaviors Directed Toward Individuals

OCB-O   Organizational   Citizenship Behaviors Directed Toward Organization

LMX   Leader Member Exchange

Abstract

Organizations are paramount places to observe human behavior. Principally, when it comes to organizational citizenship behavior, the ultimate understanding is residing inside work establishments. The present study was dedicated to discern the interconnections between employees extra role behaviors and factors behind the realization of these actions. Based on that, due emphasis was given to see the prediction capability of socio – demographic characteristics of employees, Organizational identification, Job involvement, Organizational justice dimensions on employees OCB & its dimensions in the Secretariat of the Ethiopian Parliament, as it is one of the major government organizations. The study followed a quantitative approach with correlational design. The data were collected using standardized measurement scales by taking 202 (N=417) employees as participants through probability sampling assumptions. The collected data were analyzed using descriptive and inferential statistics corresponding Percentage, Mean, Man-Whitney & Wilcoxon tests, Pearson's Product Moment Correlation, MANOVA, Regression Analysis as well as Canonical Correlation Analysis. Giving that, participants did not generally varied by their socio demographic characteristics in displaying OCB, but with the exception of their Age groups and Educational status to show Altruism & Conscientiousness patterns respectively. Work experience was also relatively a good predictor of employees overall OCB level. Organizational identification of employees was significantly correlated with overall OCB and Altruism, Conscientiousness, Courtesy & Civic-virtue dimensions; Job involvement was also significantly correlated with OCB & all the five dimensions; from Organizational justice dimensions, distributive justice was not significantly correlated with overall OCB of employees but with Altruism & Conscientiousness dimensions, Procedural & Interactional justice were significantly associated with overall OCB & Altruism, Conscientiousness, Courtesy and Civic-virtue. Overall, the proportion of variance explained by independent variables were found to be significantly fit to predict OCB in different level. From the case in point, organizations are expected to be considerate of their employees' psychological cohesion, involvement and fairness insights to enhance extra role behaviors and succeed.

Keywords: Organizational Identification, Job Involvement, Distributive Justice, Procedural Justice, Interactional Justice, Organizational Citizenship Behavior

Chapter One

Introduction

1.1 Background of the Study

Organizations are very much reliant upon their workers that are encompassed from the behavior of individuals' stand-in as participants (Steve & Thomas, 2008). Demands in an organization are fascinatingly multifaceted and interactional. Principally, from the human behavior aspects, level of different variables and the effect they brought to the survival and sustainability of that organization is a critical approach in research and development.

As a result of the diversities of organizational man power, the importance of studying the perceptions and behavior of employees in order to intensely understand the whole process of the organization based on human issues is vital. In this regard; the capability of employees to identify their organization and scale it up to create oneness to it, the actual involvement that the employees exercise towards the job they are dealing with, the perceptual process of employees' contextualization of fairness in relation to the duties and responsibilities of both the organizational workflow and decision making as well as the justification behind it are conceptually important factors to predict the general tendencies of employees' to willingly participate in their sector and try to contribute to fulfill the realization of potential outcome.(e.g. Moorman, 1991; Rioux, & Penner, 2001; Fassina , Jones & Uggerslev, 2008; Podaskof, Podaskof , MacKenzie, Maynes,& Spoelma, 2004 etc)

In organizational contexts, peoples' categorization of themselves in accordance with what they are supposed to be treated as the member of some groups and other social identity related explanations are conceptually an integrative part of Organizational identification (OID), Job involvement (JI), perceived Organizational justice (OJ) and Organizational citizenship behavior (OCB). For instance, as the context of this paper, a specific form of group identification in a likely relation with the organization they work for is imperative approach (Bartels, 2006). Similarly, diverse studies in ranges of organizational behavior revealed that the connections between Organizational identification and other interrelated self-concept variables with that of public sector employees' organizational citizenship behavior is dependably significant(e.g Dong & Sue, 2015; Karaolidis, 2016;Flávia, Fábio & Ana, 2017).

In addition, the role of employees' involvement in their routine job process is another psychological source to presume the positive outcome of the interaction of the workers with their organization. There are cases that could lead to consider involvement as an important factor in an organization; in many situations, individuals that displayed high amount of involvement in their duties perceived their jobs as essential part in everyday life and the discomposure or preference about their own characters has an inclination to be closely linked with how they are capable to attain their careers (Chughtai, 2008).In this regard, there are evidences that demonstrate the predicting influence of Job involvement to OCB in different respects of public services(e.g. Shaggy & Tziner, 2011; Seyyed, Mohammed & Kamil, 2013; Rustam, Farhad &Abdolmajid, 2014; Nwibere, 2014; Saxena & Saxena, 2015).

The option of perceived organizational justice has also a repercussion in the enablement of important accomplishments in an organization. Social psychologically, justice can be looked at as a juncture of people's objective conditions, the impression of their apparent realities, the way they emotionally react towards and of course the behavior they are shown (Hegtvedt, 2006).In organizational environment, the role of perceived justice is very critical. Organizational justice (OJ) research point out the real-life consequences of employees' treatment in a fair fashion. This issue could be extended to the employees' perception of unfairness that could lead to exhibiting a smaller amount of positive results as well more inclination to display undesirable attitudes and behavior (Paddock, Stephen & Layne, 2005). Furthermore, Organizational justice (OJ) has a great benefit to derive with great trust and commitment, further progressive job performance, deliberate citizenship behaviors and etc (Russell, David & Stephen, 2007). In relation to that, numerous studies were done and came up with different results in order to show the relationships of organizational justice components and OCB as most of them inclind with a positive bond between the two variables (e.g., Jafari & Bidarian, 2012; Iqbal & Tasawar, 2012; Mathur & Padmakumari, 2013; Nandan & Mohamed, 2015; Ali, 2016))

At an outcome level, organizations must capitalize much to the citizenship behavior among their employees if their target is to promote efficiency and success; because Organizational Citizenship Behavior (OCB) has an effect on the productivity of workforces and may possibly allow to encourage the likelihood of internal alliance (Saigon, Himmet & Muhammet, 2013). In general, organizational behavior is accompanied with the entire organizational effectiveness, which is the central sign of workplace behavioral significances (Saxena & Saxena, 2015). In this context, the idea of organizational citizenship behavior is eligible with three critical facts; first and foremost, the subject of OCBs' is not associated with the formal task or job description rather it is very essential to notice that they are accomplished by the choice of the person as an employee, following to that OCBs' are not enforceable and finally OCBs' are assumed to be positively donated to the complete success of the organization (Saxena & Saxena, 2015).

In relation to the span of the public sector, workers are fit into numerous occupations in government organizations, however, there is no major clues of exactly how employees' connection to their occupation have an impact to their attachment to the organization they belong(Hassan, 2012). Based on the less prominence assumed to the public sector in an organization – employees attachments and extra performances that are vital to the survival and realizations of both of them, the need to examine and generate a better understanding of public employees Organizational identification, Job involvement, Perceived organizational justice as predictors of Organizational citizenship behavior is potentially a right deed due to its implication on the constructive outcomes of psychological attachment regarding an essential component to workplace.

With respect to the Ethiopian context, the study of organizational related behavioral and perceptual factors is inadequate. However, there are few findings concerning the role and influences of organizational behavior variables like organizational citizenship behavior, perceived organizational justice, Job involvement, organizational commitment, job satisfaction, organizational culture, organizational climate and etc. Nevertheless, these studies are not significant from the magnitude and scope of research problems in the area.

To recapitulate some of the research findings, for instance, Yohannes (2016), made known that the OCB activities of teachers in Bahir Dar town contrasts in different dimensions like work experience, level of education, teacher characteristics (personal goals, commitment, responsibility and economy), the nature of the teaching profession, empathy for students and communities and love for one's country found as basic reasons to display OCB behaviors. In a related study, Eyerusalem (2016) ariticulately indicated the role of equity perception (justice) a in the federal public sector ministries concerning performance management system and its link with organizational commitment as well as practices, as the end result showed peoples perception of fairness in performance management system has a positive relationship with organizational commitment and inversely related with the declining level of perceived organizational justice feeling of employees.

In another turn, Temesgen (2014) found that organizational commitment components show different levels of prediction of behavioral outcomes, i.e. OCB and employes's turnover among employees of Ethiopian public universities. Woldemedhin, (2015) has also shown that job rotation practice towards employees in the Commercial Bank of Ethiopia positively moderated and boosts motivation, commitment and job involvement. Getahun and Lehal (2015) observed the importance of OCB to increase social capital among employees of the Ethiopian Electric Power Corporation in north western regional offices, especially Amhara regional state and revealed that OCB has a significant relationship with social capital.

Missaye, (2016) discussed the role of perceived organizational justice in Health care workers, in public and private hospitals, as her study found both types of workers from these sectors has low sense of fairness towards some dimensions of organizational justice and high in other dimensions especially for private sector workers(interpersonal and informational justice dimensions). Missaye has also found that Organizational justice perceptions and job attitudes (job satisfaction and organizational commitment) has a slight difference in public and private health organizations and even as strong predicting power of Perceived organizational justice on job attitudes and turn over intentions of workers (Missaye, 2016).

Furthermore, the study of organizational behavior related variables are very important strategy in order to show the psychological factors behind the stability and complexities of employees' behaviors and perceptual tendencies. However, even if there are more studies in a global level, the distribution and proportionality of these research findings did not show the needs of some regions like ours. In this regard, the aim of the current research is to assess the dynamics of organizational behaviors in relation to factors that are believed to predict extra role behaviors in organizational contexts.

Generally, different studies have tried to illustrate the influences of the research variables not in a comprehensive scope as it is put in the current study but with different dimensions. In this regard, the current study tries to combine different predictor variables as to show the actual influence they brought to OCB. Based on that, the purpose of this study is to clearly show the prediction tendencies of Organizational identification (OID), Job involvement (JI), Perceived organizational justice on Organizational citizenship behavior (OCB) in the public sector with special emphasis on employees of the Secretariat of Ethiopia's Federal House of Peoples Representatives (SHOPR) which is one of the largest public organizations in the country.

1.2 Statement of the Problem

Organizations are dependent entities on their employees' performance and extra role behaviors that are essential to overall accomplishments. By that, the study of organizational behavior plays its unique role to understand the patterns and consequences of different actions that are related to organizational citizenship behavior (OCB) and effectively communicate with employees. The dynamics of OCB are considered to be interconnected with a variety of employee behaviors. For instance, the actions of OCB may not be foreseen from the nature of works or positions of employees. On this occasion, employees who behaved in an OCB are not at all times the highest performers, but the subject of task performance is considerably interacted with OCB (Zhang, 2011).

With regard to OCB related existing research, there are variety of information which are helping to conceptualize and empirically prove the construct. In this regard, different studies were conducted especially in the western world as a means to accumulate knowledge in the area. However, there are vacuums in the context of our country, especially on OCB and its relationship with other organizational variables. That is why it makes the present study an important investigation. Because there are evidences that demonstrated the actual relationships and the need to study such variables in cross cultural contexts (e.g, Qureshi, Shahjehan & Saifullah, 2011; Akintayo & Oyebamiji, 2011; Haridakis, Robyn & Paul, 2008).

The research gap in this area is apparent when it comes to the Ethiopian context. Few scholarly works have been done in this context. Particularly, there were no significant studies that are predominantly concerned with organizational variables and their interlinkages with one another. As opposed with the western contexts, the emphasis given to the extra role behavioral patterns in the organization is not enough to our environment. However, it's posssible to fill the gap by conducting different research like the current one. Because it is very crucial to understand the real relevance of organizational behavior variables locally as most of the studies in OCB and related organizational attitudinal factors are culture bound. The majority of these studies have been conducted in the United States and Western Europe up in recent years and because of that, research conclusions are limited and to their definite cultural and socio- economic domains (Ertürk, Yılmaz, & Ceylan, 2004). As far as the role of culture is concerned, formations of what makes people to demonstrate extra role or citizenship behavior be at variance across cultures (Michele, Miriam & Zeynep, 2007).

Moreover, the concern of this particular study is also to observe combination and separate effects of different predictor variables, i.e. Organizational identifications , Job involvement, Distributive justice, Procedural justice, and Interactional justice perceptions on Organizational citizenship behavior and its dimension. Previously, this was not common to study such variable mixtures in our contexts because it would take rigorous conceptual and empirical analysis. The current study has also been uniquely featured employees work related perceptions which are evidenced to bring efficiency and extra role behaviors in different cultural contexts. As most of the research findings specified, in competitive situation organizations efficient employees whose determination should go further than customary job descriptions and official duties; citizenship practice of employees must come at this point to let them display, advanced levels of enactment and expected to do more while they are treated impartially in their place of work (e.g ,Saigon, Himmet & Muhammet, 2013).

Furthermore, the current study variables were subject to different evidences especially in relation to OCB with and in diverse contexts. For instance, within organizations, individuals lean towards modifying the degree of Organizational identification owing to the stay and character of interaction between the employee and the organization, and this could lead to the idea that more contact among employees and considerable period spend at an organization is more liable to identify themselves with it (Ufuk & Nejat, 2015).OCB is expected to be fulfilled with Organizational identification attitudes.

On another side, as earlier studies disclosed Job involvement is changing with individual characteristics such as age, education, sex, tenure, need strength, level of control and values(e.g Rabinowitz & Hall, 1977). From these points of view, individuals OCB are interlinked with job involvement in such a way that the strength and tendency of its position may to some extent fluctuate with different levels. In this regard, several studies revealed that job involvement has a direct effect on Organizational citizenship behavior (Chughtai, 2008).

Organizational justice is also an important predictor of different work related attitudes and behaviors, for the reason that it relates to employees to determine whether reasonable treatment of their jobs affect other work related variables (Liliana, Claudio & Bernardo, 2014). In this case, OCB as an extra behavioral functioning is supposed to be associated with organizational justice, because partly the perception of employee treatment in an impartial or partial way might be connected to the comparison made both within the organization or outside of it (Hassan, 2002)

Likewise , the role of socio demographic variables is also an important factor in this study to see the relationships with OCB.In this regard, there must be an extensive study with different contextual backgrounds because different studies came up with different results. For instance, recent studies have shown that Gender and OCB have relationships with different dimensions, as some of these points out the expected behaviors of men and women are slightly differing in taking part different dimensions of OCB (Francis, 2014). In another study, for example, Malek(2012) examines the relationship between gender, age, educational level, recruitment status, length of service with the organization, tenure, job classification, and intention to be leaving the service among lecturers in community colleges as well as the overall impact of demography in OCB and found different results. Others were also looking at the relationship between educational level and marriage status of employees with organizational citizenship behavior (OCB). In such studies for instance, some of them were failing to see any significant relationship between those demographic variables and OCB(Francis, 2014).

In addition, this study aims to create links between the characteristics of organizational citizenship behavior (OCB), such as personal, interpersonal/group and organizational antecedents which are the limitations of many studies in the area. The major feature of this research is its inclusiveness of different organizational behavior variables to predict one major extra role behavioral pattern. The limitations of other research in the area emanates from lack of directing a full picture out of different antecedents in the study variables. This study is unique in its essence, because the major emphasis of it is directly related to the idea that deals with key variables in the area to holistically determine the research questions in demand.In this regard, As Yutaka (2015) assessment, empirical research trends in extents of OCB is mounted in different countries and it is considered to be a major motion in areas of organizational behavior. In order to largely see the influence of different variables on OCB it needs a cautious choice of both the researcher and readers in the area, as many of the research findings focus on behavioral associations between organizational variables.

The major difference of this study is that, it encompasses important levels of psychological factors in organizational surroundings multidimensionally with overall combination of varibles.For instance, Organizational Identification (OID) is linked to Job Involvement (JI) because the two variables are more of indicators of person – organizational connections. And perceived Organizational Justice (OJ) is the best indicator of the individual's perception of fairness in organizations which is the base for behaving in both pro - organizational or hostile - organizational contexts; all these variables are assumed to predict extra role behaviors (OCB) in an organization.

In general , the need for empirical research on organizational related behaviors is essential, particularly in contextually unique cirumstances. Based on that, the basic issue in this study is to fill the gap between major attitudinal factors of employees' perceptions in organizational settings by seeing their effect on OCB. In this regard, the research title of this study is unique in its combination of variables and to the linkage it attempts to observe.

1.3 Objectives of the Study

The major objective of this study is to examine SHOPR employees' Organizational identification (OID), Job involvement (JI), Perceived organizational justice (OJ) as predictors of Organizational citizenship behavior (OCB). Moreover, in its specific spectrum, the study looks at the following objectives:

1. To explore the relationship between SHOPR employees socio-demographic characteristics (Gender, Age, Work experience, Educational Qualification, Income) and OCB

2. To examine the relationship among SHOPR employees Organizational identification, Job involvement, Organizational justice and OCB

3. To understand the combined influence of SHOPR employees Organizational identification, Job involvement, Perceived Organizational justice on OCB

1.4 Research Questions

1. Is there significant relationship among SHOPR employees' Socio-demographic characteristics and OCB ?

2. Is there significant relationship among SHOPR employees' Organizational identification Job involvement, perceived Organizational justice and OCB ?

3. Are the combined proportion of variances explained by SHOPR employees' Organizational identification, Job involvement, perceived Organizational justice significant to that of Organizational citizenship behavior (OCB)?

1.5 Significance of the Study

The current study has a remarkable impact for the understanding of public sectors' employee organizational dynamics and it contributes to create a better strategy for the promotion and facilitation of positive organizational behaviors in general and extra role behavior of employees in its particular sense.

Conducting this study has also been advantageous to those who wish to elaborate on ideas which are discussed in relation to the study variables. Especially the consequence of the independent variables would be taken into account for instigating employee centered reinforcements to scale up their performances and increase efficiency in work activities. Interested bodies on the subject could be benefited to manage human resources they have, with respect to psychological factors in working places that are directly held accountable to boost and even to minimize Organizational citizenship behaviors (OCB).

For the target organization, if the findings of this study are properly realized could bring important opportunity to understand the approaches of employees there and dealing with the future organizational behavior aspects in an advanced management style. Besides, the core behavioral attributes of the study population will be discussed with the communicating process of the paper. In this regard, both employees and the leadership of the organization would get an important lesson to see the implications of the study results and the consequences they brought in real organizational settings.

Finally, the process and findings of this research are helpful to the researcher himself, other interested readers, the organization in concern and to the dissemination of knowledge and practices in the area at large especially in our age, because the impact of employees' attitudes in a day to day basis is a critical concern. It is also creating a unified understanding of organizational behavior aspects and relationships they have with the role and responsibilities of employees and organizations at a mutual level of analysis.

1.6 Scope of the Study

The current study is concerned with the investigation of Organizational identification (OID), Job involvement (JI) and Perceived organizational Justice (OJ) as predictors of Organizational citizenship behavior (OCB) in the Ethiopian public sector, with a special emphasis on the Federal level organization.

In its depth phase, the characteristics of organizational related variables have a huge impact on the behavior of employees, and the study of larger area may be favored in terms of coverage. However, this study's aim is to show the relevance of organizational behavior dynamics in different organizational setting with varieties of effects. To deal with it, the selected organization which is The Secretariat of House of Peoples Representatives of FDRE (SHOPR) is believed to give enough information regarding the study of research problems.

With this assumption, the implication of public service organization's involvement in their employees overall behavioral and attitudinal dynamics is the manifestation of these organizations effectiveness and efficiency. Based on that, the study looks at a specific scope in the above mentioned organization with a detailed account of seeking to understand employees' psychological preparedness to engage in OCB. In this context, the study focuses on only the staff of SHOPR with the predicting role of different variables to see the effect they brought in employees OCB.

Generally, this study is only analyzed with the scope in one public sector organization at a federal level. In this regard, the study overlooks different organizational contexts from the comparative perspective and has no intention to overgeneralize for the country's public sector employee attributes. The major purpose of the study is to contextualize the effects of different independent organizational behavior related variables in an organizational basis. For this to achieve, the scope is considered to be sound to discuss the implications of different behaviors and perceptual patterns in the organizational environment. This is directly resulted in predicting the performances of employees with their power of engaging in extra role behavior in the respective organization. It is important to understand the study variables effect in a large organization like the target one in the current study.

1.7 Operational Definitions of Concepts

Socio - Demographic Characteristics: For this specific study it represents employees Social and demographic related factors that are serving as independent variables to determine the relationship with the outcome variable of the study (OCB). In this study, these characteristics are Gender, Age, Work experience, Educational qualification, Income.

Organizational Identification (OID): For this particular study, this concept is considered as employees' individual psychological feeling that is based on the sense of oneness to the organization they are working with. There are cognitive & affective aspects within this construct. The variable is measured by Meal & Asforth, (1991) scale.

Job Involvement (JI): This concept is another dimension for the employees attachments to the organization, which is measured based on the amount of exertions employees invested in their respective job positions for this study. (As this particular study concentrated on, Job involvement could be seen with different perspectives: as an individual characteristics, situationally determined variable and as a product of person – situation interaction (Rabinowitz & Hall, 1977). With regard to measurement , Kanungo,(1982) scale was used in the current study.

Perceived Organizational Justice (OJ): For this particular study, employees' perception of fairness towards their organization's activities both in the process, decision making, informational and instructional patterns with other colleagues.(The process of organizational justice as the current study concentrated on having the following dimensions, namely: Distributive justice as measured by Prince & Muller (1986) scale; Procedural justice as measured by Sweeny& McFarlin (1997) scale; and Interactional justice as measured by Niehoff &Moorman(1993) scale.

Organizational Citizenship Behavior (OCB): It is employees' behavioral patterns that are voluntarily done as an extra role activities in an organization and are not included in the formal job description of workers. The availability of this behavior is predicted from different independent factors and has a possibility to promote and minimize based on the potential factors influenced it. (OCB has the following 5 dimensions designed for measurement in the present study, namely: Altruism, Conscientiousness, Sportsmanship, Courtesy and Civic-virtue).Concerning the measurement tool, Podsakoff et.al (1990) scale was used.

Chapter Two

Review of Related Literature

2.1 Introduction

Because of the complexities of the study constructs, the first part of this chapter gives an account to the detail clarification and understanding of predictor variables of the study in accordance with theoretical perspectives. In this regard, the basic concepts of Organizational Identification (OID), Job Involvement (JI), Perceived Organizational Justice (OJ), as an independent construct and in relation to OCB. This is done to provide an overall representation of the study variables, with the nature, characteristics and organizational relevance as an attitudinal and behavioral existing factor. The development of organizational analytics in discussion on this study has considered both the holistic aspects of important variables and their respective dimensions and components.

In the second part, the presence of OCB that is reflected in everyday life are elaborated on with its essence and formal application. Major conceptual backgrounds and its linkage with the utilization of the construct in an organizational context will be highlighted in accordance together with theoretical and empirical discourses. The major aspects of OCB are parts of this segment to be discussed with relevant relationship with the study.

At last, conceptual framework of the current study will be drawn based on different theoretical and conceptual analysis regarding the interlinking between the independent and dependent variables. In this instance, the hypothetical assumptions of the writer of the paper, the abstraction of the nature and significance of research problems to objectively predict the interaction of particular constructs in the study will be depicted.

In sum, this chapter gives a comprehensive outlook to the study variables as a potential disposition of understanding the fundamental tendencies of the current research insights. Evidences from varieties of sources are integrated to satisfy the literature demand of the study in creating both the conceptual and empirical explanations. With this task, the literature review part of the study has targeted to assess the critical characteristics of the study variables with having the context of the study in mind.

2.2 Theoretical Foundations of Employees' Attitudinal and Behavioral Patterns in an Organization

Organizations are one of the recognized places to nurture human potentials and work productivity. In this regard, the availability of organizational members, especially a different group of peoples or teams is turning out to be manifestations of human interactions. Because, the idea of human beings at work together can be comprehended in alignment with basic human nature, attitudes and psychological needs (Micheal, 2001). In this context, different theories are assessing the nature of human beings in relation to organizational settings.

For instance, identity theory assumes human beings as having a free will to define the situation as an actor; that can identify important things and act upon the best attention of those identifications and their aspiration to be fit with the construction of identity as well as the action they are taking are being checked to be congruent with others in the condition which they are anticipated to bring about their goals(Stets, 2006). For a person to give an emphasis on the context in relation to organizations or other places, the equilibrium between his/her attitudes and probable behaviors in the situation has an important role; because it is not always likely to show the fullest parts of attitudinal predispositions in action. This is happened to win out the norm of appropriate behavior expectations with that of peoples attitudinal patterns(Gilovich, Keltner, Chen & Nisbet, 2016).

Social identity theory provides additional explanation to the person –organization relationships and the essence of human identity. For this theory, individuals mange to keep their social identities by assuming the group they belong to other groups, particularly the comparison of their own group positively than that of the other group(Tajfel & Turner, 1986). Relying on the social context, different traits like sense of duty, modesty or patience importantly defines personal identity and social identities(Verkuyten & Wolf, 2002).Depending on such theoretical explanations employees perceptions of their internal work environment or intra organizational cues play a pivotal role to influence their identification with the organization they are engaged in (Lam, Liu & Loi, 2016).

Self- categorization is another important cognitive perspective which is an extension of social identity of peoples and the reason of why the formation of these identities be presented and explained in terms of the cognitive process. This theory asserts that, in different decision making process groups tend to identify with their group membership and tries to build contextually appropriate and identity- determined or consistent group standard; the proposition of this theory, therefore varies from social identity theory in a way that the former seeks to higher order group process of group behavior in its up-and-coming level in order to predict the swing in self-perception from self- categorization elements of individual identity to categorizing self in relation to social identity(Hogg, 1999; Wicklund, 1999). However, the influence of organizational life cannot be attributed to behavior to the organization unless one can be defined that the organization is psychologically 'real' to the subject with different regards(Ickes, 1999).

Social exchange theory has a different social-psychological way of explaining employees' attachment to their organization in general and the need for attitudinal and behavioral patterns in particular. The basic tent of this theory is the assumption that, the fundamental interaction of humans is depending upon the exchange of social and material resources(Murdvee, 2014). Based on that, variety of interactions could be anticipated accurately as the theory emphasized (Griffin, 2011). Research and theory in this context have shown that, the link between social exchange theory and OCBs are eminent. Especially from the views as individuals presumed to originate a cognitive evaluation of the current situation and matched it using the standard fairness which help them whether to engage in OCB or not (Pierce & Maurer, 2009).

Finally, the explanation of fairness in the organizational contexts better understands by the equity theory and its preceded explanations as the way to facilitate the components of organizational justice behavior.In the equity theorizing, people are motivated to achieve fairness or equity with the exchange process in terms of outcomes they be given comparative to the contributions that they deliver (Donovan, 2001). In sum, a theoretical origin used for a relationship concerning fairness and citizenship was drawn from equity theory as well as other principles of social exchange(Moorman, 1991).

2.3 Organizational Identification

Research in organizational behavior has attempted to deliver imperative theoretical combinations of key writings in the organizational sciences, and appropriate investigation and challenging analyses of persistent organizational concerns and problems (Stow & Kramer, 2003). In relation to that, Organizational identification has considered for longer period as an important and critical construct on different literatures of organizational behavior (Ashforth & Mael, 1989).

2.3.1 Basic Conceptualizations

Albeit organizational identification is originated from social identity and symbolic interaction theories, contemporary notions underline a social identity whereby organizational members classify themselves and others centered on roles and involvement in an organization or work division; symbolic interactionism, as a feature of interpersonal relationships, is not often theorized or empirically assessed in studies of organizational identification (Jones & Volpe, 2010). As Organizational identification is a wide concept that scholarly trends and research interests are various. For instance, pioneers of this conception like, Ashforth, Harrison & Corely(2008) has demonstrated the major questions related to the understanding of Organizational identification;including the nature of identification,with a range beginning narrow to wide-ranging formulations and differentiated positioned identification from deep identification and organizational identification from Organizational commitment, try to link the discussion between individual and organizational outcomes as well as numerous organizational behavior themes.In this regard, as a meta-analysis by Riketta (2005)found, first, it is emperically supported that organizational identification has associated with work related attitudes, behaviors and context variables, second, it was clearly identified that the connection between Organizational identification and Organizational commitment is emperically separate and finally,different scales of organizational identification could bring about much diverged results.

Moreover, Ashforth, Harrison & Corely (2008) have also refers a process model that consists of set of sense breaking and sense giving which interacts identity and sense making as well as creating identity accounts, they also emphasized on team, worker group and sub unit: relational; occupational; and career identifications as well as how multiple identifications may encounter, come together and combine in organizational settings.These speculations are adding to the notion of organizational behavior dynamics at large in terms of the psychological factors that bind employees to their organization. Because, understanding the psychological relationship between the individual and the organization consequently of great theoretical and practical significance used for research in organizational behavior (Knippenber, 2006)

Organizational identification has a tremendous impact to the description and prediction of behavioral and attitudinal factors in organizational context. It also has a valuable proposition to explain individual attitudes and behaviors as well as individual and organizational identities. In this regard, a meta analytic review by Lee, Park, & Koo, (2015), shown that Organizational identification is considerably related with basic attitudes like job involvement and related constructs as well as behaviors   like extra- role performance (OCB) etc. In organization; organizational identifications direct effect on general behavior far more than general attitudes and they also clearly showed an organizational identifications tendency to be moderated by national cultures and high level social context to which the organization is found in as a means to the variations of individual response in terms of its stronger effect to collectivist culture like ours than in an individualistic one. Specifically in relation to national cultures, Lam, Liu, & Loi, (2016), found that the effect of collectivism as a moderator to extra- role behavior and organizational support through organizational identification.

Organizational identification's conceptualization has been subject to diverse outlooks with which the frame of understanding its nature may vary. However, there are pertinent points to holistically assume the construct. For instance, organizational identification occures when people integrate beliefs of organizational identity in to their own individual identity.In this case people became challenged to identify with different figures comprising organizational leaders,symbols, mission statements, products etc to cerate a strong beleif; in other direction, organizational identification encompasses social aspects of individuals ideniy or self concept and identification consists of the nature of perception of value congurence to individual and an organization but not all the times and the value in the organization not necessarily cause a drastic changes in individual values (Pratt, 1998).

2.3.2 Organizational Identity and Identification

Organizational identity and identification are core constructs in organizational phenomena and organizational arrangements which they convey distinctiveness and oneness (Albert, Ashforth & Dutton, 2000). These constructs partake a tremendous influence on numerous organizational behaviors and consequently on the working of an organization and the realization of its objectives. (Jong & Gutteling , 2006). Organizational identity frequently is represented as that which is essential, distinguishing, and persistent about the character of an organization (Gioia , Shultz & Corely, 2000).

Organizational identity generally refers to what participants perceive, feel and think about their organizations (Hatch & Schultz, 1997). In organizational identity, there are foundational thinking that brought the concept to be conveyed by perspective of individuals which is treated as an organizational identity as an analogue of individual identity; these functions, drawing attention to those individual and collective social actors and distinguishing structural features of individual and organizational identity referent that are parallel to each other (Whetten, 2006). On the other hand, there is no one agreeable distinctions between organizational identity and identification in research, however, these two constructs takes in common that are understanding how individuals perceive and classify themselves as members of a group and the organization or a larger incorporating community (Ravasi & Rekom, 2003). Organizational identity has played an important role in organizational dynamics; it impacts leaders and members together within an organization and organizational members are also influenced by an organization's identity (Lin, 2004). In relation to this condition, organizational identification has claimed to have an exceptional importance in explaining personal attitudes and behaviors in organizations, as it encompasses the critical characteristics of components as individual and organizational identities (Lee, Park, & Koo, 2015). Overall, both identities (individual and collective) and identification in its process bound people together in organizations in the case of personal and shared accounts that people author in their determinations to create sense of their world and deliver meaning in their lives (Humphreys & Brown, 2002).

2.3.3 Major Components of Organizational Identification

In organizational perspective, there is an ongoing argument in the literature to what way organizational identification (OID) has to be theorized and operationalized (Edwards & Peccei, 2007). However, there are important components in the construct of organizational identification. Especially as its purpose entails individual and organizational effects as well as quite a lot of links to common organizational behavior topics (Ashforth , Harrison, & Corely, 2008).

A) Cognitive and Affective Components

Because individuals often identify with groups in order to either reduce apparent uncertainty or to feel better about who they be present as personalities. In this regard, Organizational identification has two components; cognitive and affective. Cognitive and affective identification are two distinguishing forms of social identification in organizational settings (Jhonson, Morgeson & Hekman, 2012). Cognitive identification can be defined as the thoughts or beliefs regarding the extent to which individuals define themselves on the basis of a social referent; whereas affective identification as the feelings individuals experience about themselves in relation to the social referent and the value they place in that social identity(Johnson & Morgeson, 2005).

Research has provided an evidence of cognitive identification that it consistently predicted by cognitive ability, organizational prestige and neuroticism, in relation to that affective identification is predicted from prestige and extraversion as well as these two components are delivered predictive validity of organizational commitment, organizational involvement, and organizational citizenship behavior(Johnson & Morgeson, 2005). In related studies, it shows that   perception of organizational support values in individual basis is determined by self concept components of cognitive identification as organizational attributes and an affective tie that bind individual employees and the work organization (Xenikou, 2014)

2.3.4 The Relationship between Organizational Identification and Organizational Citizenship Behavior

As various studies revealed, people who very much identify with their organization are more likely to perform OCB (e.g ,Kane & Perrewé, 2012;Choi , Moon & Kim , 2014). Accepting the correlation between such variables will benefit both public and private segments of organizations about the role of organizational identification and organizations must to recognize that OCB are helping behaviors backing significantly to organizational effectiveness (Srivastava & Madan, 2016). Organizational identification has different aspects that serve as differentiators interlinked with work related attitudes and behaviors(Dick, Wagner, Stellmacher & Christ, 2004). In organizational level of extra-role behavior the performance of organizational citizenship behavior has been directed to individual level of analysis in most of the early research traditions, but recent research traditions have focused on the group level or unit-level OCBs and the intervening instruments as well as boundary situations of the interactions among OCBs and unit-level outcomes(Podaskof, Podaskof, MacKenzie, Maynes & Spoelma, 2014). In this case, the role of organizational identification plays an important role both at individual and group level, as it positively encourages employees' organizational citizenship behavior and it also contributes to an intermediate function between organizational justice and organizational citizenship behavior (Ganglion, 2011). In Particular, related research shown that organizational citizenship behavior has a tendency to be affected by organizational identity and self concepts that it is possible to strengthen and improve such variable contribution in order to increase OCB(Allameh, Alinajimi & Kazemi, 2012). Moreover, Organizational identification is considered to be amongst the major and key element to employees ties in organizations and make them committed to the organization, that makes the variable as many studies verifies its positive contribution to organizational citizenship behavior (Demir, 2015).

2.4 Job Involvement

The concept of job involvement deals with the amount of employees' effort to identify themselves with their present job, which attracts research interests in empirically oriented psychologists (Gilkar & Darzi, 2013). It has involved as a crucial aspect to an organization's success and it leads to improved satisfaction as well as better productivity for the organization (Abdallah, Obeidat, Aqqad, Al Janini & Dahiyat, 2017). Equally job involvement demands an employee's willingness to work; those who are willing to working hard can be considered as highly involved individuals and less willingness creates low involvement of the job as the concept includes employees cognitive preoccupation on the job, engaging in action and the concern they develop to one's job(Sharma, 2016). This shows that, individuals' effort to be involved in their job has an impact to incur satisfaction of several salient psychological necessities to which the effect will be reflected at organizational basis(Wrk, Bosohoff & Cilliers, 2003).

2.4.1 Basic Conceptualizations

Job involvement as a psychological construct has long been conceptualized in different ways. For instance, as Kanugo(1982) critically assessed early conceptualizations of job involvement that carries exessive meanings and these can be identified by; first,the construct overlaps with intrinsic motivation ,second most past researchers take a mixed up position on the anticedent situations of job involvement using the matter of identifying the state of job involvemet and its consequent effects , third job inolvement conceptualized by early researchers with a failed understanding of distingushing the two situations in which an individual can demonstrate personal involvement,namely specific for particular job context and generalized work context.In any case, literatures have not been adequetly adressed the role of job involvement in precise (Ho, Oldenburg, Day & Sun, 2012). In accordance with the basic tenets of job involvement, however there is research support, including the role of individuals to decide response at work which emphasized the importance of work as it is considered by individual believers and the value of work to form part of individual identity or self cocept;in this regard gob involvement as a factor to influence employees live, eat and breath the job (Govender & Parumasur, 2010). In related to the fact that job involvement is an important concept, it is favorably encouraged other related aspects of the job like OCB and likely become committed to their organization(Nwibere, 2014). However, there are theoretical distinctions between job involvement and work involvement; that work involvement stands for a normative belief of work in an employee's life and is a function of historical, cultural conditioning and socialization, where as job involvement serve as personal character that is based on one's satisfaction (Kanugo, 1982). In different contexts, the conceptualization of job involvement is varied accordingly towards individual and circumstances as well as the disagreement to its meaning would be resolved through conceptualization of the concept (Antil, 1984). However, meta analysis and review by Brown (1996) clearly supports that, job inovolvemtnt is influenced by personality and situational variables, it has a strong correlation with job and work attitudes, there was little difference in the measurements of involvement relations as well as there he found a modest and systematic differences among the studies of public and private organizations towards job involvement. In sum, previous research in the areas of job involvement capitalizes on its importance to affect individual and organizational outcomes (Ekmekçi, 2011). There are also related research findings that job involvement might consider a person to further socialize by the organization and it enhances the employees' objectives to advance levels of work performance & quality of employees' lives at work (e.g Beheshtifar & Emambakhsh , 2013; Rizwan, Khan & Saboor , 2011).

2.4.2 The Relationship between Job Involvement and Organizational Citizenship Behavior

Job involvement is considered to be a useful predictor of OCB, as some of the study findings in the area shows direct or indirect relationship between the sub scales of OCB and job involvement (e.g Diefendorff, Brown, Kamin, & Lord, 2002; Shragay &Tziner, 2011). In specific terms, for instance, other research findings have shown that OCB in the organization could cause up to 52% of job involvement of employees and it plays an important role in organizational performance of employees (Vijayabanu, Govindarajan, & Renganathan, 2014). In this regard, the prediction cababiliy of job involvement is positive and significant among its effects on OCB. (Behtooee, 2016). Concerning the area of public organization, extra-role behaviors are more available and intensive than that of the private organization (Pavalache-Ilie, 2014). To substantiate this argument, the findings by Mirzaee & Beygzadeh (2017), gives an important implication as it is shown that the employee job involvement in the government tax office can be explained 78% of OCB dimensions in the Iranian context. Other cross cultural studies indicated that there is a positive effect of the affective and behavioral involvement of employees on some OCB dimensions and cognitive involvement inversely influence helping behaviors as well as these effects were partly qualified by employee job category and gender (Yutaka, 2012). In relation to gender, there are consistent trends with some findings that sex is indeed moderate parts of the job involvement and OCB relationships which have evidence of the strong relationship between the variables and females than males (Diefendorff, Brown, Kamin, & Lord, 2002). In extended research on the mediated role of job involvement, it has considered to be one of the factors to predict the relationship between OCB, emotional exhaustion and diminished personal accomplishment (Chiu & Tsai, 2006). In related research job involvement has also a Positive mediated role in job characteristics and OCB. (Chen & Chiu, 2009). Job involvement research has also revealed that, it has a direct and positive effect on OCB; in relation to this among the leadership styles transformational leadership has a significant influence on job involvement as well as personality can be a major indicator of job involvement(Dwirosanti, 2017). Generally, job involvement affects OCB in such a way that high involvement is increasing the probability of extra role behaviors; study in this regard has shown that, involvement partially mediates among organizational justice and OCB and suggested that to advance employees OCB employers has two primary encourage employee job involvement (Safe, Kojuri, Badi, & Agheshlouei, 2013). On the contrary, there are previous studies that are indicated that involvement in decisions leading employment practices could only contribute to a small but indirect effect on OCB (Cappelli & Rogovsky, 1998).

2.5 Perceived Organizational Justice

Organizational justice can be explained as employees' perception that are related to workplace procedures, interactions and outcomes to be fair in nature; the extent to which these perceptions avail attitudes and behavior in their differentiation which impact on the performance of employees and organizational achievement (Baldwin, 2006). In particular, the concept of organizational justice encompasses the employees' determination of whether they have been treated fairly in their jobs and the influence that is brought by these determinations in the work-related variables (Moorman, 1991). In this case, the issue of justice or fairness has concerned all individuals; concerning the issue, justice dimensions have long been demonstrated, but theoretical ways that can cause this effect are not well identified (Judge & Colquitt, 2004). In research, justice is perceived to be a socially constructed variable (Colquitt, Colon, Wesson, Porter & Ng, 2001). Research has shown that employees' perceptions of distributive, procedural and interactional justice could contribute to the availability of key work outcomes, including performance, job attitude and citizenship behavior(Rupp, 2001). The concept of justice in terms of its effect to other related variables is indeed a most important issue because it matters is more or less identical by means of preserving that individuals care about the way they are treated by others (Folger & Cropanzano, 1998). Its effect has also reached into not merely determining organizational performance, but also the economic well being of an employee and it could balancing employer employee relationships (Yean &Yusof, 2016). In general, organizational justice in its context is mirrored by several different aspects of employees' working lives (Colquitt,Greenberg & Zapata-Phelan , 2005)

2.5.1 Basic Conceptualizations

In organizations, justice results are contingent on whether one's consequences are fair and correspondingly on degrees of procedure and treatment (Lind, 2001). The discussion of organizational justice is concerned with individuals as they relate to what they achieve with those achieved by other colleagues, however the insight of justice has not only limited to the comparison of outputs (Bayarcelik & Findikli, 2016). Furthermore, in the study of organizational justice has stipulated three reasons that it, first includes the social phenomenon related to features of social or organizational life, second, it considers each organization's human resource as a main asset, thirdly employees behavior and treatment will have a tendency to affect their future attitudes and behaviors (Jafari & Bidarian, 2012). In research traditions, the concept of justice nowadays focuses mainly focuses on employees care about justice (content theories), the process of fairness in its processes and peoples responses to perceived injustice (process theories); justice research continually directed on the multilevel stage that has turn out to be concentrated on how shared perceptions of justice create with in work group or organization as well as how these perceptions and its reaction to it has differed throughout cultural contexts including organizational and national cultures (Rupp & Thornton, 2017). In Addition to that, justice conceptualization in organizational literature has focused on the three main trendes;differenciation which is deliberate on the idea that justice conceptualization can be seen as interactively with additional justices dimensions that are up to, be segmented into different sources in advance, the cognition trend postulated on the rational and calculative issue which is part of the paramount justice theory, the exogeneity trend conceptualized justice as its independent variable position in most empirical theories (Colquitt, 2012). In general, different researchers on organizational context have revealed the best benefit of organizational justice in an organizational context for the realization a of organization vs employees nexus(Iqbal, Rehan, Fatima & Nawab, 2017). From such aspects, organizational justice has a tendency to be effectively predicted OCB, that is if there is a higher state of justice perceptions there will be a higher probability of showing OCB with a good standing relationships among employees (Jafari & Bidarian, 2012). In general, research in organizational justice and its perceptual propensities has been conceptualized in different perspectives and empirical investigations, that are contributing to the development and understanding of the concept in alignment with organizational behavior related variables.

2.5.2. Dimensions of Organizational Justice Perceptions

The perceptions of organizational justice, broadly comprise from procedural and relational components; the previous one is concerned with decision making activities and their participatory tendency to different pursuits within the organization in the input, consistency, accuracy, correctablity and ethical considerations, and the later is imposed on the considerably and fair treatment among individuals in their context (Elovainio, Kivimäk & Vahtera, 2002). In this regard, organizational justice can be seen as with specific dimensions, such as, distributive justice, procedural justice, interactional justice perceptions.

2.5.3 Distributive Justice

Distributive justice has conceptualized in terms of the perceived fairness of outcomes and many of the predictions this variable has been related to its strong importance to organizational contexts that have depended on the distribution of outcomes in general (Cohen-Charash & Spector, 2001). In work places distributive justice is an emphasis on employee treatment in its utmost properties; that includes discrimination of employees, the fair- share of employees in   promotion for some and marginialization for others with the tendency to be connected with top management and ethos (Yadav &Yadav, 2016). Distributive justice could be elevated in situations that are having consistent outcomes in which equity and equality of allocation of things could be managed with implicit norms (Srivastava, 2015). Moreover, the concept of distributive justice is thoroughly related to reward distribution in organizational contexts.

In theoritical explanation the concept of distributive justice can be best described three important schemes; first relative deprivation theory, which is focused on the socio economic status of peoples to compare themslves with others interms of jugding the situation they are found in that had been very much included in psychologcial literatures in distributive justice related conceptualizations,Second, social exchange theory is concentratiing about the fairness of exchanges between peopless relations including justice that are even determined future relations amonge them with the expectation from past relationships,third, equity theory is another imporatnt notion which is focused on the value of ratio of out-comes and in-puts of ppeoples in organization incomparison with the coworkers that comprisesof perceptions of fairnes and coluld lead to inequity distress (Seo, 2013).

The perception of distributive justice has been a critical viewpoint because of the employees' nature of seeing the concept of fairness with partiality, that is outcomes and resources are not allocated with the same quality and quantity in terms of pay/salary, job status, and etc (Mathur & Padmakumari, 2013). Furthermore, the idea of fairness is noticeable especially when decisions are regarded to be made with limited resources that are causing both decision makers and peoples to be concerned with fairness (Bertolino, 2006). In conclusion, distributive justice has orientated to be a major factor for its predictability capability to cognitive, affective, and behavioral responses to specific consequences (Cohen-Charash & Spector, 2001)

2.5.4 Procedural Justice

In organizational perspective, procedural justice encompasses the process of allocation of outcomes with no intention to the obtainability outcomes themselves and it is a vital element to keep institutional legitimacy when decisions are affecting individuals and can definitely cause certain outcomes (Colquitt, Baer, Long, & Ganepola, 2014). The concept of procedural justice was first developed from studying fairness of formal procedures governing decisions that are the basis for individual perceptions (Masterson,Lewis, Goldman & Taylor ,2000). As the consideration of procedural justice is comprehend on the process of decision making, procedures in organizations are free to be set up and there still are differences in the procedures used to address same important questions (Lind & Taylor, 1988). In relation to that, the procedural justice contribution to workplace is pointing to for work attitude and performance of employees in that;ressearch support, procedural justice can increase the presence of organizational identification and it revolved the influence of moral identity centrality on employee engagement (He, Zhu , & Zheng, 2014).As an important notion, Procedural justice was first conceptualized in early theories like Levental et.al introduced six important determinants of procecedural justice judements;consitency of appliying with a time and space congurence, taking accounatabllity freeing from bias especially from the interference of the third party, accuracy of information to put al decisions with enough evidence, using some alternative mechanizms to correct inacurate decisions,be loyal to moral and instrumental standards of ethics and be open to the participation of important bodies or peoples that are percived to be or actualiy affected by the decision (Colquitt ,Colon ,Wesson , Porter , Christopher & Ng ,2001).These conceptualizations are important indicators of the value of procedural jutice and its implication in organizational context.

2.5.5 Interactional Justice

Interactional justice is concerned about the dignity of people in relationships in the area of in an organization, which is an addition to procedural justice that is giving emphasis to the way management of an organization is showing conduct to their employees or recipients of justice (Cohen-Charash & Spector, 2001). In short, Interactional justice is a recent conceptualization in justice literatures with which the development of organizational justice theory has an impact in its development and heavily relying on (Xie, 2016). With regard to interactional justice, fulfillment criterion, researchers like, Bies has identified respect and neutrality in serving as rules and truthfulness and justification in other side as the guiding principles to its success (Hegtvedt, 2006).Interactional justice may sometimes confused with procedural justice, but as Lonsdale,(2013), suggetsts the relation ship between this two variables has a clear conceptual boundary between the organizational and supervisor level of analysis; that is procedural justice more strongly attached with organizational level variables and interactional justice with supervisor related variables like leader – member exchange and organizational citiezenship behavior focused on individuals in relation with one's supervisor.However, supervisor related justce perceptions are explained vairances in citizenship out comes better than organization-originated justice irrespective of the target they are focused in (Colquitt, 2012). The major characteristics of interactional justice are that they are unaffected by the individual self- interest and the tendency of its perceptions is interactional justice (Ladebo, 2014). Furthermore, interactional justice could be extended into sub two sub components: informational and interpersonal (Usmani & Jamal, 2013). Informational justice is the examination of peoples truthfulness and it is about the justifications of things with an adequate explanation in cases which generates wrong things, on the other hand, interpersonal justice has focused on the relationship between peoples in the justice process that whether they are treated with dignity (Cropanzano, Bowen & Gilliland, 2007). In sum, interactional justice is a very powerful construct that give a very good insight to explain organizational justice dynamics throughout the entire organizational processes and outcomes (Bies, 2015). In general, some theories, predicted that employees' perception of interactional injustice may be resulting in a negative reaction towards the organization and concerning specific outcomes (Cohen-Charash & Spector, 2001).

2.5.6 The Relationship between Organizational Justice and Organizational Citizenship Behavior

In organizational settings, the availability of organizational justice has a great impact to generate organizational citizenship behavior (Jafari & Bidarian, 2012). In this regard, the state of organizational justice has an important role to positively predict both organizational identification and organizational justice and the interplay between the two (Guangling, 2011). In broader respect, the dimensions of OCB are all positively related to additional factors in organizations an towards work in general (Tziner & Sharoni, 2014). Among the dimensions of perceived organizational justice, there are early evidences that supports the value of interactional justice into predicting the occurrence of citizenship behaviors (Moorman, 1991). Other researches were also shown the effect of distributive and procedural dimensions of justice in relation to OCB, that culture and gender has also has been seen with different to these variables (Farh, 1997). The quality of overall fairness is influencing the dimensions of organizational citizenship behavior as some studies like, Tansky(1993).On the other hand, leadership training of organizational justice for members of a certain organization has a tendency to increase positive justice perceptions behaviors in both the leadership-member relationships (Skarlicki &Latham, 1997). In recent decades, as a meta-analytic study shown, interactional and procedural justice perceptions are found to be a strong predictor of OCB (Fassina, Jones & Uggerslev, 2008). And other researches have proven the significant relationship between distributive and interactional justice in relation to OCB (Awang & Ahmad, 2015). Moreover, manager trustworthiness could contribute to the variation in the explanation of OCB other an above than interactional fairness (Cobra & Lim, 2007). Additionally, in theoretical respects, the concept of justice and citizenship behavior has been primarily drawn from equity and other social exchange theories (Moorman, 1991). Finally, the dimensions of organizational justice have different level, but the influence to organizational outcomes, including OCB (Jawahar & Stone, 2016).

2.6 Organizational Citizenship Behavior

Organizations are not always the formal task oriented entities, rather they also depend on voluntary activities such as task completions that are based on positive and helpful social behaviors which are not bounded by time or personnel inconvenience that are not intended to getting any opportunities or further benefits (Bez, 2010). In this regard, the concept of organizational citizenship behavior is an instance that is comprised of different dimensions and the cumulative effect of these dimensions are indeed very important to create an astonishing influence on organizational operations and effectiveness (Organ, 1988). As construct OCB is important in organizational contexts that could not be explained by different things like same inducements that prompt entity, conventionality to contractual role prescriptions, or high production (Smith, Organ & Near, 1983).

2.6.1 Basic Conceptualizations

Among the major conceptualization of organizational citizenship behavior in terms of the dimension was proposed in 1980's with the scholarly papers (e.g, the works of Smith, Organ & Near 1983; Organ 1988; Organ & Ryan, 1995;Podsakoff, Ahearne & MacKenzie, 1997; Organ, 1997). On the essential characteristics of the construct, there are concrete evidences that supports the strong relationship of OCB (Altruism, Civic-virtue, Conscientiousness, Sportsmanship, and Courtesy) and different predictors like those to be studied in this paper as many scholars reflected (e.g. Le Pine, Erez, & Jhonson, 2002). In its conceptualization the construct is comparatively new to other organizational behavior concepts (Bukhari, 2008).

The major conceptualization of OCB is focused on the extra role behavior of employees that are performed by outside of the contracts and with a non- obligatory manner (Organ, 1988). But the conceptualization has even changed in by even Organ (1997), that he asserts the considetaion of OCB as an extra role behavior, outside the job and unrewarded by the formal system is not adequate. However the in most situations, these behaviors are not rewarded or reinforced by the organization as a formal job achievements. The explanations of these behavioral patterns are distinctly seen in the formal role and extra role activities that can easily distinguish what is expected of the organization and free standing contributions (Lo, 2009). In this regard, the best explanation of OCB is included that; first, its action may or may not be compensated in the future, but the action in this regard might be included in the formal reward system of the organization; Second, the action of OCB has a great impact to cause organizational effectiveness (Organ, 1997).

In different studies including a meta-analytic review by Organ& Ryan (1995) which referred 55 studies in areas of OCB, shown that diverse job attitudes are vigorous predictors of its presence. These attitudinal factors are helpful to effectively create optimistic and productive act of employees that are heavily based on the wishes of those individuals to support other workers and their organization in general (Shanker, 2014). In general, all the conceptualizations of OCB focus on employee behaviors that are supportive but not critical to the task or the job which can encompass behaviors like helping co-workers and involving in functions outside of the formal job description (Lee & Allen, 2002). And the construct has strongly linked to many predictor variables with behavioral and attitudinal predispositions and these relationships are also true to the dimensions within OCB (LePine, Jeffrey, Ertiz, Amir, Johnson & Danie, 2002).

2.6.2 Dimensions of OCB

OCB can be performed in both individual level and team level: the former is mostly characterized by secluded behaviors and the other is more observable and could be reinforced by team members and it created shared acceptance and anticipations as well (Nelson & Hrivnak, 2009). In this regard, the dimensions of OCB are served as to measure the individual and team patterns in the actual presence of the construct and its relations with other organizations related variables. In accordance of dimensions, various theoreticians have developed different ranges that they could be reflected in the overall scale of the OCB measurement. That may create a confusion over the conceptualizations of OCB dimensions, as the rapid growth in research on the area overlaps with the nature of the construct (Podsakoff, MacKenzie, Paine & Bachrach, 2000). In relation to the dimensions this research focuses on the five dimensions outlined by different scholars, but with more emphasis by Organ (1988) before and after the further development of the construct.

2.6.3 Altruism

These are actions that constructively contribute to help other persons in day to day work problem by instructing those individuals who are new to the organization in different situations like by showing the way to use materials, support co-workers to catch up with work types, fetching for another co-worker materials which are not accessible to the worker (Organ, 1988). It is primarily introduced to point on individuals with the considerations of groups by increasing individuals' achievable (Jahangir, Akbar, & Haq, 2004). In general, altruism is concerned with the helping style of members of the organization (Chahal & Mehta, 2010)

2.6.4 Conscientiousness

It represents the awareness and performances of individuals in organizational contexts, that are beyond the least possible necessities like, timekeeping, housekeeping, wise use of resources and maintenance related activities (Organ, 1988). This dimension also has a tendency to boost the capacity of individuals and groups in an organization (Jahangir, Akbar, & Haq, 2004).

2.6.5 Sportsmanship

This dimension concerned about the ability of individuals to show citizen-like posture in relationships with others by tolerating the inconveniences that are foreseeable and the capability of peoples to accept the burdens of work without complaining and whims (Organ, 1988). The presence of this behavior has a positive impact to enhance the constructive effects of the organization and times spend to achieve this task (Jahangir, Akbar & Haq, 2004)

2.6.6 Courtesy

The best explanation of this dimension comes from individuals' attainment in showing considerable gestures for others to prevent problems and contacting (keep in touch) with people to reduce actions that have negative consequences to people and it also includes giving an advance notification about work schedules to peoples who require them (Organ, 1988). If courtesy is achieved helps to prevent problems and enables effective use of time (Jahangir, Akbar& Haq, 2004).

2.6.7 Civic virtue

It is focused on the actual and active political participations of employees in the internal organizational context that could consist of expressing one's opinion and carefully reading the sending & received mails, be present in the meetings, well-informed to organizational issues at large(Organ, 1988). This is concerned largely on both the interest of the individuals and the organization as well (Jahangir, Akbar & Haq, 2004). Moreover, the responsibility of individuals to participate and show a meaningful concern is helpful to bring about the existence of the organization(Chahal & Mehta, 2010).

2.6.8 Antecedents and Consequences of OCB

Organizational citizenship behavior as a construct treated with different patterns such as comparing peoples that are having high in their functioning related to OCB and those who are showing less performance in OCB. These studies are focused on OCB as the dependent variable to observe the factors that are known to affect the presence and consequences of OCB (Alizadeh, Darvishi, Nazari & Emami, 2012). Moreover, the variety of studies that are providing the domain of OCB in accordance with the effect they brought to organizational performance (Chahal & Mehta, 2010). According to studies in the area, especially from public sector settings, the Occerance of OCB is known to be affected by gender, age Marital status, personality factors and organizational climate (Suresh & Venkatammal, 2010). Some Other research has been showing that leadership-styles like servant leadership and procedural justice can strong predictors of OCB (Ehrhart, 2004). These conditions largely known as antecedents of OCB.

A) Major Antecedents of OCB

The relationships of different attitudes and behavioral factors are complex in their nature. Dependent on the interplay between such variables and OCB sometimes been stronger and in other dimensions they could be loose; for instance a meta analytic review of the area showed that, OCB has a strong relationship with job satisfaction, in role – performance, perceived fairness, organizational commitment, leader supprotiveness as well as differences in this case dissimilarity in subject groups and work settings be registered not registered as the cause for much variation in the correlation between those variables (Organ & Ryan, 1995). Generally, as a predisopstion and antecceedent the major factors to influence OCB are including to consider both the environment and personal context (Harper, 2015). Moreover the research tradition on OCBs are focused largely on the four classifications of antecedents, including, individual (employees' characteristics), task characteristics, organizational characteristics, and leadership behaviors (Podsakoff, MacKenzie, Paine & Bachrach, 2000, *p.* 526). However, these antecedents of may differ across cultures (Gelfand, Erez & Aycan, 2007). In general, studies in OCBs are more concerned with understanding the factors that cause employees to achieve it (Jex & Britt, 2008).

From individual characteristics the role of socio-demographic variables is very important. Nevertheless, there is no generalizability to the influence it has on individual OCBs. As research in the area with different studies does not guarantee the prediction of such variables on OCB (Qureshi, 2015).However, previous research found that race and age, sex dissimilarities are factors that may affect OCB in general basis (Chattopadhyay, 1999). There are also research findings that support the effect of educational level (educational qualification) and employee's length of services as a means to get into helpful behaviors including OCB in an organization (Pavalache-Ilie, 2014)

According to research, from the major personalities, the big five personality traits are important antecedents. In this regard four of which, namely: extraversion, neuroticism, agreeableness and conscientiousness are found to be correlated with OCB with a weak bond however (Zhang, 2011). Nevertheless, A meta-analytic review showed that the five factor model of personality traits is indeed predicting stronger than job satisfaction and the relationship between each personality traits are significantly varied with inducing OCB (Chiaburu, Oh, Berry, Li, &Gardner, 2011). Furthermore, personality is recognized as a disposition factor that is studied using different dimensions OCB with direct and indirect effects (E.g Suresh &Venkatammal, 2010;Ilies, 2009). In other hand, as Li, Liang & Crant (2010) revealed, proactive personality and organizational citizenship behavior have a   strong correlation that is effectively moderated by procedural justice perceptions.

Attitudinal factors are another important factors to predict OCB. These factors include; job satisfaction, motivation, organizational commitment, employee engagement and the level of trust are measured by attitudinal patterns and the relationship with OCB is a significant indicator (Zhang, 2011). Employees with more positive attitudes see OCB an in role behavior which gives them to act on citizenship behaviors and role description effect; in this case employees attitudes and their citizenship may also increase with their definition of OCB as an extra role (Tepper, Lockhart & Hobber, 2001). On the other hand, the availability of OCB is less strict than in-role performances to be limited with ability and work process (Organ & Ryan, 1995). Some studies are supported the role of different attitudinal patterns like job satisfaction and organizational commitment; in this regard, these variables are positively related to OCB while there is no abusive supervision in organizations (Tepper, Duffy, Hoobler, & Ensley, 2004). In general, as meta - analysis demonstrated there is a strong and

Furthermore, received organizational justice perceptions are an important antecedents of OCB. The influence they are having is also well researched (e.g. Moorman, 1991). Some studies also show the effect of organizational justice in direct and interactive process, especially the procedural justice type and its influence on the basis of individual differences that brought about

OCB role definitions (e.g Kamdar, McAllister, & Turban, 2006). In accordance with justice perceptions and their relationship between other work related variables, the research has proved that procedural justice, climate could be affected together with positive service climate employees' commitment to supervisors to aid them with having OCB (e.g Walumbwa, Hartnell, & Oke, 2010). Moreover, the effect of interactional justice is also eminent among employees' intentions to perform OCB and other organizationally attached helpful actions (Willi & Zainuba, 2002)

Similarly, role perception can be taken as the one of the major antecedent of OCB and it includes role conflict, role ambiguity and overload that are proved to be negatively associated with OCB and job satisfaction (e.g Jahangir Akbar & Haq 2004; Eatough, Chang, Miloslavic& Johnson, 2011). But role perceptions could be also positive, for instance, as a meta-analysis revealed that there is a positive and direct relationship between role overload and OCB (Eatough, Chang, Miloslavic & Johnson, 2011). An earlier study that was done across four countries (USA, Australia, Japan, Hong Kong) samples on this regard has shown that, job roles may be differs between supervisors and subordinates to perceive some dimensions OCB as an expected part of their job (Lam, Hui, &Law, 1999)

Motivation is also one of the antecedents of OCB, as research shown, for instance proscial value motives are very much correlated with OCB than other motives, especially focused on individuals OCB-I and organization based motives are stronger than other motives to come up with OCB-O as well as the variance in individual differences on OCB may also be explained by motivation (Rioux & Penner, 2001).

Besides, the relationship between leadership characteristics and OCB is significant in different contexts (Jahangir Akbar & Haq 2004). A meta-analytic review of the area clearly indicated that OCB has a moderately strong as well as a positive relationship with LMX (Ilies, Nahrgang, & Morgeson, 2007).

Finally, group membership and features are important antecedents to behave in discretionary manner that includes OCB. In this regard the working group norms are being traditionally helpful to establish OCB in an organization (Ehrhart & Naumann, 2004). Some studies were also indicated that elements of OCB (helping behavior and civic virtue) are partially a function of the characteristics of performance feedback that group members be given (Bachrach, Bendoly& Podsakoff, 2001). In addition to that leaders have the ability to enhance the group OCB in an organization; in that the leaders exercise of OCB in turn would lead to result group OCB in promoting the action towards members (Yaffe, & Kark, 2011). Moreover, Group level, helping behaviors (OCBs) would be decreased in the case of membership variety in gender and education of individuals (Choi, 2009).

B) Consequences of OCB

OCB is a powerful indicator of different organizational and individual related consequences. In relation to that, as a meta -analysis proved, material ratings of employees of performance, different withdrawal-related criterion, like absenteeism employees' turnover intentions and actual turnover as well as reward allocation decisions could be included as an individual related consequences of OCB; on the other hand efficiency, productivity, customer satisfaction reduced cost, unit level turnover is among the organizational outcomes of OCB (Podsakoff, Whiting, Podsakokoff & Blume, 2009). However the consequences of OCB are slightly differing across cultures; in relation to that, positive emotions, continuance commitment and work place social inclusion that is attributed as consequences of OCB in a cross cultural context like the USA and China especially in hospitality an tourism industry employees (Ma, Qu, & Wilson, 2013). In another dimension, citizenship motives that are included pro-social values, organizational concern and impression management could influence OCB that it in turn contributed to employees' job performance ratings, citizenship fatigue and workplace status (Klotz, Bolino, Song, &Stornell, 2017). In a different context, OCB may have its own negative impact on task performance that is caused to lower performance, which is targeted to be given a lower performance appraisal as well as less reward which could affect employees who are behaving responsibly and exchange based OCB(Zhangq, Liao, & Zhao, 2011). In general, OCB availablites including its consequences are more prevailing in public organizations compared to private ones (Pavalache-Ilie, 2014).

2.7 Conceptual Framework of the Study

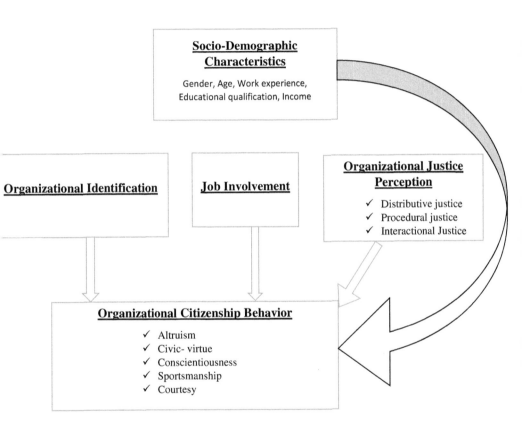

Figure -1- Conceptual framework of the relationship between Predictor and Outcome variables of the study. (That are extracted from different literature reviewed by the writer of the paper)

2.8 Summary

As the conceptual and empirical discourses in different areas of organizational behavioral patterns attributed, the contents of the current chapter has tried to specify the major connections between the study variables in terms of correlational aspects and the bond that they are associated with different dimensions. The main implication of such abstractions is indeed a founding basement to generally conceptualize the major study variables and related dispositional factors that are directly or indirectly related to the outcome variable to support the research questions and predictions

The major philosophical conceptualizations that are supported what was meant to be addressed in this regard is a real challenge in a sense that it passes through rigorous reasoning and casual relations among the dynamics behind the rationalization of the study factors in general. More precisely, the writer of the paper has concentrated on creating a space to clearly state the natural relationships surrounded by different scholarly impressions on the subject as well as the outcomes that is believed to be grasped from research traditions.

Furthermore, the basic intent of this chapter was featuring to digest the critical components of the study in relation to vast literacy resources that are hence to substantiate the ideas of the study in terms of objectivity and sound argument. That it will continue as a defense to make a bridge between the major objectives of the study and its logical connection with the results of the study.

Overall, the present chapter discussed the most important properties of Organizational identification, Job involvement, perceived Organizational justice and Organizational citizenship behavior as to the value of their application and the interplay between each and every variable across disciplines in Industrial-organizational and social psychological explanations and the nature of such variables throughout their interdisciplinary landscape. Trends of research in the area has been developed with continuation of the adjustments of the characteristics and components of the study variables with strong influences from different perspectives and theoretical foundations. The achievement of the chapter is counted on the synthesis criterion that inclusively managed to deliver a conceptually robust explanation for the mastery of integral part of the study as a whole.

Chapter Three

Methods

3.1 Introduction

In this section, the major parts of how the study is directed in terms of the specific and detailed manner will be provided. The conceptualization of the study variables are putting to noticeably show study participants procedure, measurement & calculations, data analysis as well as ethical considerations and etc to be applied in the case of the current study. As American Psychological Association (2010) asserts, the methodologies of studies may differ in the content and the form, but each part of the method delivered a full description that contributes to the reader in appraising the relevance of the methods that are evidently shown the reliability and validity of outcomes.

3.2 Research Design

The principal design of this study is based on a non-experimental quantitative research. Correlational research design is selected as a tool to interconnect with the purposes of the current study. As Appelbaum et.al, (2018) indicated, in such research designs there is no intention to manipulate variables; the major task for these studies is to observe, classify, describe and analyze the naturally occurring relations between variables of interest (*p*.13). The basic approach to conduct correlational research for this specific study is found to be discovered in terms of the quantitative nature of the variables. Not that all the computing concept is fundamentally quantitative in nature, but as a measurement categorized, the major predictors and their functional outcome are examined with relationships and the association they are formed in considering the fact that the scales are discussed.

In the development of this research process, the concerns of proposing variables are to discover their interrelationships among themselves and within the sub - dimensions. In this regard, the computed value of such correlations is to exactly observe the associations that are demonstrated while interacting with the conceptualization each variable. The findings of this research could be a clear indication of the quantifiable results of the study in relation to the research questions that are addressed within the conceptual framework.

Generally, the correlational research design is a match to the current study in order to bring valuable result summarized with the basic purpose of the study. Regarding to that, the power of the study design is decided by the real mixture of variables in such a way that the effect that was determined out of their calculation. Hence, it is very essential to characterize the validity of such results in statistically sound techniques.

3.3 Study Area

The study area for this research is Secretariat of The Federal House of Peoples Representatives of Ethiopia (SHOPR) and employees that are rendering professional and administrative support to the House. The area is found in the capital city Addis Ababa, Arada sub city, surrounded by 4 kilo district, especially found in front of the Office of the the the Ethiopian Prime Minister. According to the FDRE constitution, Article 55, powers and functions of the House of Peoples' Representatives are different in their nature. The secretariat is re-established by proclamation No. 906/2015 of the Federal Negarit Gazette to effectively execute the objective which is to provide professional support and administrative service to the House of Peoples' Representatives in order to effectuate its constitutional responsibility. (*P*. 8261). Moreover, the employees of this organization are expected to be effective and efficient for the making of provision of services in general. The SHOPR divided into twelve directorates and fifteen working teams that facilitates the powers and duties of the secretariat in varieties of service based chains. The target population of this study is ultimately taken from this organization's employees and the responses are believed to be reflected the organization's status in relation to the current study variables.

3.4 Population and Sample

The population of the current study is covered the total active employees of the Secretariat House of Peoples Representatives of the FDRE which is 417 in number. The population of this organization is involving in providing professional support and administrative services necessary for the effectiveness of the legislative, supervision and oversight, and representation mandate of the House of Peoples' Representatives; render general professional and administrative service to the House of Peoples' Representatives and to its committees and other internal organs; administer the Federal Negarit Gazette; perform public relation services to the House of Peoples' Representatives; ensure institutional memory; provide library, research, information and documentation services to the organs and members of the House of Peoples' Representatives; undertake capacity building activities, provide minute recording, hall, publication and other conference services to the House and its organs; provide transport service to members and organs of the House and etc.(Federal Negarit Gazette, proclamation No. 906/2015). Moreover,the population size is calculated around different numbers due to new recruitments and turover from the organization. As well as with different reasons that are taken into consideration to unbiase the data taking process to specifically seek an equal chance of selection to inclusively represent the population in the study process. The aggregate population of the organization is divided among directorates and by gender of the participants to proportionally administer the data selection process. The description of population patterns in relation to the sampling process and precision criteria will be fully provided in detail in the next sections.

3.4.1 Sampling Procedures

For this specific study proplablity sampling procedure is used to determine the study participants sampling determinism. With regard to that, stratified random sampling and simple random sampling procedures are being used to substantiate the selection of the sampling process. The rationale behind these sampling procedures is inclined into the important points. First, as the population of the organization staratified in to some tewelve directoriates which are believed to be composed of homogeneous groups at least in their professional and work categorization, Second, from each stratum the sample will be determined through the simple random sampling procedure with an advantage of giving impartial change for the selected participants and the directories they belongs. Third, it facilitates the proportional allocation of samples from each stratum and the gender of participants in the strata. All the advantages of assigning these sampling procedures will certainly be part of the study sampling criteria. The sampling frame of the population of the organization is available to the researcher in this case and it is not that much complicated to assign what is appropriate as sampling standards to validate the student demand

As the total population is known for this research, the sample size is determined by Yimane (1967) formula. In this case the overall participants of the study are getting an approximate chance to be included in the sample size in terms of the general probability assumptions of this sampling formula. Moreover, according to this postulation the precise sample size will be determined as follows:

Formula, $n = \dfrac{N}{1+N(e)^2}$

Where, n= is the sample size   N= population size e= margin error

According to this the total active population of the study organization is 415, with the researcher's decision of the margin error to be 5%.

$$n = \frac{417}{1+417(0.05)^2} = \frac{417}{2.04} = 204$$

The general sample size is, 204 in this study, but assuming different inconveniences from the respondent's participation in the study a possibility of 10% of the sample will be added as a sampling size. This would make the total sample to be 224.

In light with this research's sampling assumption, the probability of proportional representation in each stratum's population is determined by the given calculation of stratified random sampling in simple terms as;

$$\textbf{Sample size of the strata} = \frac{\textbf{size of entire sample}}{\textbf{population size} * \textbf{layer size}}$$

Based on that, the table that shows how proportional data is taken from different straums in the organization and gender composition within each of those directorates will be provided below:

Table-1- Stratified random sampling model of the current study

No	Name of the Directorate	Directorate Number of people in each stratum	Gender		Total number of People in the Sample
			Male	Female	
1	Legislative,Oversight and Supervision	114 $\frac{224}{417*114}=61$	51 $\frac{61}{114*51}=27$	63 $\frac{61}{114*63}=34$	61
2	Procurement, Finance and Property management	29 $\frac{224}{417*29}=16$	11 $\frac{16}{29*11}=6$	18 $\frac{16}{29*18}=10$	16
3	Human Resource development& management	132 $\frac{224}{417*132}=71$	41 $\frac{71}{132*41}=22$	91 $\frac{71}{132*91}=49$	71
4	General Service	64 $\frac{224}{417*64}=34$	47 $\frac{34}{64*47}=25$	17 $\frac{34}{64*17}=9$	34
5	Communication Affairs	20 $\frac{224}{417*20}=11$	16 $\frac{11}{20*16}=9$	4 $\frac{11}{20*4}=2$	11
6	Information communication	13 $\frac{224}{417*13}=7$	8 $\frac{7}{13*8}=4$	5 $\frac{7}{13*5}=3$	7
7	Government Whip	9 $\frac{224}{417*9}=5$	3 $\frac{5}{9*3}=2$	6 $\frac{5}{9*6}=3$	5
8	Research and Capacity building	4 $\frac{224}{417*4}=2$	1 -	3 $\frac{2}{4*3}=2$	2
9	Women and Child Affairs	3 $\frac{224}{417*3}=2$	1 $\frac{1}{3*2}=1$	2 $\frac{2}{3*2}=1$	2
10	Audit & Inspection	4 $\frac{224}{417*4}=2$	2 $\frac{2}{4*2}=1$	2 $\frac{2}{4*2}=1$	2
11	House of Speaker and the Secretariat main office	13 $\frac{224}{417*13}=7$	9 $\frac{7}{14*9}=5$	4 $\frac{7}{14*5}=2$	7
12	Planning and Reform	12 $\frac{223}{417*12}=6$	5 $\frac{6}{12*5}=2$	7 $\frac{6}{12*7}=4$	6
Total		417	195	222	224

Simple random sampling method is the final way to select participants out of the strata. In this case the process of this technique is utilized in accordance with a random number as an initial starter to proceed with the other descriptions that are included to randomly select all the participants under each stratum and categorization within directorates and gender. Moreover, this is done on the basis of calculating each stratums population as it is divided by the sample of each stratum to identify the first number as a random initial cut off point. Example, to select an appropriate sample of participants from Legislative, Oversight and Supervision directorate within the gender composition of the directorate is used by the random number table as a common way to produce random samples.

3.5. Measurement and Instrumentation

In the current study, the variables are measured with different levels to get a relevant response in relation to the quality of the data. To deal with that, there were stages that were done by the researcher with the consideration of scientific methods utilized on the behavioral studies.

3.5.1 Description of Variables

The major variables for this study are provided in the following patterns:

A. **Independent (predictor) variables** – These variables are very crucial to compare the variables in their predictive power.Socio demographic characteristics of respondents, Organizational identification, job involvement, perceived organizational justice are the independent variables of the study.

B. **Dependent (outcome) variable** - Organizational citizenship behavior is the dependent variable of this study .

3.5.2 Instrumentation

In this study, there are instruments used to measure the variables and to facilitate the study measurement process. These instruments are from different sources and the quality of their measurement proved internationally as well as it also customized into the local use of this research by using methods that are helpful to see the real ability and contextualization of parts of the instruments with cultural differences

3.5.3 Organizational Identification Scale

This scale is primarily adapted from Meal & Asforth (1992) which they developed with a six items Likert scale. In general this measurement scale has provided as the most reputative and consistence to effectively see people's tendency of their identification with the organization and a sense of oneness to it. In this study the provisions of the factors to measure this specific variable are provided with a continuum from (1=strongly disagree; 5=strongly agree). The items included "When someone criticizes (name of the organization), I feel like a personal insult". All the items on this scale are coded in a same way with a direct approach without any reversely coded item. The original reliability of the scale is 0.79 (Meal & Asforth, 1992). The main important parts of this scale are being measured with affective and cognitive aspects. In this study item number, 1-6 belong to this scale.

3.5.4 Job Involvement Scale

The 10 item scale is provided to fulfill the measurement of this variable. This scale is adopted from, Kanugo (1982). The property of this scale is mainly expressed with an individual's cognitive ability to be attached to his/her current jobs. The scale is measured with Likert scale from (1=strongly disagree; 5 = strongly agree). The main items of this scale are concerned with direct coded except item number 8 and 13 in this study's questionnaire which are reversely coded ones. Moreover, the scale is included items like "To me, my job is only a small part of who I am. (R)". The original reliability of this scale is 0.82 (Kanugo, 1982). In this regard, this scale has satisfactory psychometric properties in relation to unidimensional measures and validity (Kanugo, 1982). In this study, item numbers, (7-16) are the properties of this scale.

3.5.5 Organizational Justice Perception Dimensions Scale

This construct is the byproduct of three important dimensions into it; namely distributive justice, procedural justice and interactional justice. These variables are measured with different scales by different researchers. Because it encompasses the employees' determination of whether they have been treated fairly in their jobs and the influence that is brought by these determinations in the work-related variables (Moorman, 1991). The full properties of these scales put as follows:

A. **Distributive Justice scale-** adapted from Price & Mueller (1986) with a six items, considering the amount of justice for allocation of organizational resources as a result of seeing employee responsibilities, education, experiences, and performance (Bez, 2010 *p.* 98). This scale has a direct coded items that are measured with Likert scale (1= strongly disagree; 5= strongly agree). From the items "When considering the work that I have done well, I am fairly rewarded." are included. The original reliability of this scale is ranged from .74 -. 98. These reliability scores were observed by different researchers; as .74 by Niehoff & Moorman (1993) and .98 by Moorman, Blakely, & Niehoff (1998). In this study item number, 17-22 are components of this variable.

B. Procedural Justice Scale- is measured by Sweeney & McFarlan's (1997) with thirteen items, in terms of degree of employees' perception regarding job decisions making process (Bez, 2010 p. 98). The scale is measured by a Likert scale (1=strongly disagree; 2= strongly agree). In this regard, there are items that are reversely coded (item numbers, 23, 25, 28). In sum, items from this scale includes "I am not sure what determines how I can get a promotion in this organization. (R)". Regarding the original reliability of this scale it reached from .84 - .85. That it noticed by .84 by Sweeney and McFarlin (1997) and .85 by Moorman et al. (1998). In this study, item numbers (23-35) are taken from this scale.

C. Interactional Justice scale- Interactional justice is measured by using Niehoff and Moorman's (1993) 9-item scale, the major concern of employees' perception regarding whether their thoughts and needs are considered through making job decisions. (Bez, *p.* 98). This scale has a directly coded item and it is measured by a Likert scale (1= disagree; 5= strongly agree). The original reliability of this score, extends from .92 -. 98. As Niehoff & Moorman, (1993) demonstrated .92 and Moorman et al. (1998) witnessed .98 levels of reliability coefficient. In general, in this research the items that represent Interactional justice scale are (36-44).

3.5.6 Organizational Citizenship Behavior scale

To measure the extent to which people are behaving in organizational contexts regarding extra role behaviors, the scale is selected from internationally recognized instruments. The scale used to measure this construct is based on, Podsakoff et al.'s (1990) that includes 24 items based on Likert scale formulation (1=strongly disagree - 5= strongly agree). Overall, this scale has five dimensions measured in different patterns. Namely: **Altruism, Conscientiousness, Sportsmanship, Courtesy and Civic virtue.**

A. Altruism- is composed of 5- items that are focused on helping other peoples in different contexts of the organization. This dimension has an original reliability score that reaches .67 - .91 to which different researchers like .91 by Smith et al. (1983); .89 by Organ & Konovsky, (1989) and .86 by Hui, Lam, & Law (2000). In this research the items of this dimension are from (45-49) which are directly coded. The items from this dimension includes'

B. **Conscientiousness-** is made up of five items that are additional determinations spread out the normal obligation of role behaviors. The dimension has an original reliability score of .79 as observed by Fields (2002). In this research, the dimension has represented by item numbers (50-54) that are not reversely coded.

C. **Sportsmanship** – is a five item dimension that measures the ability of individuals to show citizen-like posture in relationships with others by tolerating the inconveniences. This dimension has an original reliability of .76 -. 89 in which different researchers like Fields (2002) observed. In this research the items that are composed out of sportsmanship includes (55-59) which all the items are reversely coded.

D. **Courtesy -** is also a five item dimension that is focused on attainment in showing considerable gestures for others to prevent problems in general. This dimension has an original reliability of .69 and .86 according to Fields (2002). In this research the number of items that are put the dimension found from (60-64) in the questionnaire.

E. **Civic - Virtue -** this dimension is consists four items assessing active participation of employees in the organization that includes expressing one's opinion, be present at meetings, well-informed to organizational issues etc. As Fields (2002) the original reliability of this dimension is stretched from.66 to. 90.In this study, the dimension is found to be represented by item numbers (65-68).

All the computing variables are discussed in relation to their measurement, patterns and which assumes to observe their specific reliability and concrete evidences of how much they are being found valid in different criteria by previous researchers. In this regard, the instruments are found to be strong to measure this research variables and the interaction they will be created in order to see each others effect. Nevertheless, the real patterns of the instruments in our local context was to be tested by different mechanisms like: expert judgement and pilot test before the administrations of this instrument to the actual respondent samples of the study.

3.5.7 Validity and Reliability Check to the Local Context

As previously discussed, the study variables are internationally recognized organizational behavior constructs that are measured with standardized instruments. However, the contexts in which they are applying do have an effect on both giving and accurate and consistence response and the outcome they are intended to be investigated is indeed having an effect. To resolve this issue, the researcher tried to apply different methods that are going to get an assurance weather they study variables measurement has an anticipated effect in the area of the current study.

3.5.8 Validity

While there are different methods to check the face, construct, content, criterion validity of a specific data collection, the researcher prefers to follow the direct results of pervious researches concerning the study variables. In this case, there are important ways that must be applied in order to reassure the validity of the research variables and the measurement they are used. As Bez (2010) if one needs to decrease faults from the validity of research, it is better to administer instruments that are proven to be valid by pervious researches in different contexts, which is preferable than generating a new measurement. In this regard, the other most important thing is to consider the sampling pattern of the study in which it contributed to a well-grounded outcome; in relation to this, the researcher applies stratified random as well as simple random sampling method which is supported by a probability sampling assumption to back the appropriateness of the results for generalization and wider acceptance. On the other hand, to assure the contents of the instruments in their coverage of varieties of contexts and knowledge, the researcher tried to modify inappropriate contents, especially when it was translated into Amharic language with the help of other expert judges from different disciplines as a means to adjust the way the contents of the instruments are conceptualized without changing the actual construction of adopted scales. This is primarily done with two important points: first, the experts suggested some items to be contextualized in local flavor and secondly, the researcher himself participated in the translation of the instruments with having both the technical aspects of how the constructs apply in the local context without interfering with the basic characterizations of the instruments. For this to be done, the translation was also rechecked by a professional translator by showing the instruments as well as the translated version to critically assess the grammars and usage with a more accuracy verification. To further check the alignments of the construct and the actual measurement tool, the researcher used a self – administered questionnaire that it was proved by different researchers to measure the constructs with large number of samples.

3.5.9 Reliability

As consistence measurement instruments, the constructs in this specific research are provided with an original alpha coefficient score that are acceptable and strong in different criteria.

More on that, the current research must be supported in the measurement of the reliability of constructs with the population of the study area and other populations with similar characteristics of the study population before proceeding with the actual research investigation. This is done with different procedures in the application of the systematic reliability testing pre testing process. For this to happen, the researcher intended to engage in two important activities that believed to be facilitated the reliability checking process. They are added in the next section:

A) **Expert judgment as to prove inter- rater reliability**

To analytically see the contextualization of the research constructs, five experts from different disciplines, but related to organizational context is participated to give their judgement as they focused to automatically arrange the possibility of their speculations on each and every instrument on the basis of their expertise and organizational experience as a worker for many years. Based on that, the combination of these expert judgments as an indicator of the appropriateness of the items to measure what is intended in the current research. Moreover, the participants of this task are provided as follows:

1. A Human resource team leader who has an MA degree in Human Resource Management and more than 25 years of experience in organizational contexts and human Relation aspects.

2. A Social affairs senior research expert who has an MA degree in Developmental psychology and more than 15 years of experience in different positions with administration and other places.

3. A Human resource senior research expert who has an MA degree in leadership and more than 25 years of experience with different positions with leadership and expert posts.

4. A Communication affairs, acting director who has an MA degree in TEFL and worked as a press expert and in other positions for more than 8 years.

5. A Legal studies senior expert who has an LLM degree in Public international law with different experiences and expertise positions for more than 15 years.

As the above mentioned experts gave their judgment, the results varied in different patterns that the researcher made to be cautious in terms of properly contextualized and appropriately used the constructs instruments in a local context. Because of the results of these ratings show some speculation in terms of some items real measurement pattern in our contexts, for instance items from all the instruments has an original English grammar usage patterns which are not familiar with our context are carefully translated with concern. In other side, the responses of these raters were computed in descriptive ways, to show the variation they have scored. As result, most of the items found to be accepted by these experts, but there were cases that were not totally accepted by the judges, for example, there was a great difference in perceived organizational justice items as to whether they are really measured what is intended to measure by the instruments in accordance with the local context, and some of the judges clearly indicated that these variables are very important to measure with the selected instruments but with a careful consideration of cultural contexts. All other items and the overall instruments were critically assessed by these peoples as they are from different backgrounds and work experiences.

After all this, the researcher taking time to carefully adjust the instruments with great detail and the translation of items is also part of this consideration, especially from the point of view of assigning appropriate wordings to express what are the basic components of the each item's statement. As this process is the pre-pilot test direction, the researcher prepared all the important modifications in terms of the familiarization of the instruments in the local Ethiopian public service context before the actual administration of this instrument to the target population. In this context, the valuable indication was found from expert judgement to create a strong measurement scale of the constructs.

In sum, the rater agreement upon the scales probability of being measured what they are intended measure is almost found to be satisfactory. For instance, rater agreement on Organizational identification is about 90%, job involvement, 86%, Distributive justice, 76.7%, Procedural justice, 62.2%, overall OCB, 86% and its sub scales,   Altruism, 86%, Conscientiousness 80%, Sportsmanship 76%, Courtesy 88% and Civic virtue, 73.3% and this clearly showed that they have at least accepted what the items are concerned to measure. The account of inter- reliability   tests among all the raters in terms of interclass correlation coefficient of scores of the scales are literary diverse in its variability. In relation to this, the Organizational identification scale has the lowest agreement levels among raters which is $r(5) = .26, p = .31$, that it shows the agreement between the raters is not consistent for this scale rather it is happening by chance and reliability score earned from the raters in this regard was also very poor, $\alpha = .26$. On the other hand, Job involvement has been calculated and its interclass correlation coefficient is *being r* (5) =.91, *p* =.001, which is significant in terms of rater agreement on the scales consistency and the reliability scores of raters has *α*=. 91 it is strong in accordance with the rater agreement to measure the construct. Organizational justice scales were also examined. As the results showed that, distributive justice has an interclass correlation coefficient of r (5) =.83, *p*= .007 and it is also true that the Cronbach alpha *α*=.83 which is very strong in terms of the raters agreement's consistency, Procedural justice has been scored *r*(5)=.98, *p*<.001 and its reliability is also strong *α*= .98, the Interactional justice has also an interclass correlation of *r*(5)=.93, *p* < .001 with the Cronbach alpha of *α*=.93 that the organizational justice constructs are very much consistent in relation to the raters agreement level. Finally, the overall Organizational citizenship behavior scale interclass correlation was, *r* (5) =. 97, *p* <.001, with the total alpha level of *α* =.97 and in terms of its dimensions, Altruism has *r* (5) =.90, *p* <. 001, with *α*=. 90; Conscientiousness, *r* (5) =.94, *p* <.001, with *α*=. 94; Sportsmanship *r* (5) =. 82, *p* = 0.05, with *α*=. 82; Courtesy, *r* (5) =. 64, *p* =. 058, *α*=. 64 and Civic virtue; *r* (5) =. 85, *p* =. 033 with *α*=. 69. The interpretation of these scores was very similar in three out of the five dimensions (Altruism, Conscientiousness and Sportsmanship, Civic virtue) as the rater agreement was found to be significantly consistent. Courtesy dimension had slightly better reliability score among raters, but their agreement is not significant rather it is by chance that the raters has no homogeneity in terms of consistency.

Generally, as the raters' scores showed that some of the scales and dimensions within the study variables must be translated with greater care or considering revising. But most of the scales have strong agreement from raters with strong consistency and interclass correlation results. The researcher in this case prefers to make sure the accuracy of translation of items and be actually seen the reliability of the study variables both in the pilot and research samples. Because the study variables have repetitive reliability scores cross culturally and with a standardized research outputs.

B) Translation Process
First of all, the instruments are translated fully by the researcher assuming the know-how of the perspectives of the study variables. After this was done, the first draft of translated version was given to a professional translator who has a B. A degree in English Language& literature and currently working as senior translator, to give advice on the grammar and usage of the items

without missing the context of the instruments. The expert gave an advanced correction on some of the items translations patterns and the adjustment was made in accordance with the translator's advice and the final translated version was getting ready to be administered to the pilot test.

C) Pilot Test

After all, the process was done, the final stage of this research process before it is administered to the actual site was piloting the instruments to show the strength of the items in terms of giving a consistent outcome in different situations. In doing so, the researcher selected a similar population of respondents from a sister organization, known as Secretariat of The FDRE house of Federation, which has a common establishment story with the study area and the population of this organization shares specific characteristics of the study area in general. The pilot test was conducted on 30 respondents with a return rate of 19 samples by considering proportionality between genders and job qualifications. After analyzing the results, the subsequent items were getting very low reliability rate and adjusting to having the original flavor of the items. Generally, the test results were showing that the overall reliability scores must be taken into concern as a way to proceed with the actual study. In this regard, the scores are, $\alpha = 0.72$ (OI); $\alpha=0.50$ (JI); $\alpha=0.92$ (DJ); $\alpha=0.69$ (PJ); $\alpha=0.92$ (IJ); $\alpha= 0.56$ (overall OCB); $\alpha=0.80$ (Altruism); $\alpha=0.56$, (Conscientiousness); $\alpha=0.34$, (Sportsmanship); $\alpha=0.55$, (Courtesy); $\alpha=0.54$, (Civic virtue). In these contexts the pilot test results have clearly shown that most of the scales and sub scales of the current study variables meet the minimum requirements of the consistency with small sample size. But care must be given to the real context of some variables, especially for sportsmanship subscale of OCB. After noticing this fact, the researcher gives a tremendous action to critically revise the formats of the scale translation process and key language characteristics of the Amharic versions of the scales in relation to standardization and quality grammar usage. That is why the actual study results of reliability scores have become improved significantly by taking into account the large sample size and diversification of respondents of the study. The strong clues of the consistency of the scale in the actual study are of course the backbone of the study results reliability at large. Based on that, one can conclude that the current study has tried out all the necessary steps to undergo with essential phases of the scientific study procedures.

D) Alpha Coefficient comparison

The reliability score in relation to the original research contexts and the current ground field is compared in the next section.(Based on responses from the actual 202 samples of the study).

Table- 2- Comparison of reliability of scores of instruments in the original research and the current study

No	Instruments	The original alpha coefficient of instruments	Alpha level in the current study's final data collection
1	Organizational identification	0.79	0.79
2	Job involvement	0.82	0.74
3	Organizational justice perception dimensions	-	-
3.1	Distributive justice	0.74 - 0.98	0.92
3.2	Procedural justice	0.84 - 0.85	0.77
3.3	Interactional justice	0.92 - 0.98	0.91
4	Organizational citizenship behavior	-	0.84
4.1	Altruism	0.67 - 0.91	0.84
4.2	Conscientiousness	0.79	0.75
4.3	Sportsmanship	0.76 - 0.89	0.83
4.4	Courtesy	0.69 - 0.86	0.80
4.5	Civic- virtue	0.66 - 0.90	0.76

As the table above indicates the original reliability scores of instruments in previous researches has an acceptable level. With all the instruments applicability in this research, the tangible alpha coefficient scores in the current study were computed and the results shown that there is a respectable and a very good level of reliability in general as compared with the original level of reliability in terms of different conditions.

3.6 Data Collection Procedures

The process of data collection of the current research has been done with care. Regarding this, the data were collected in different stages and with the help of -2- data collectors recruited by the researcher. In this process, the primary duties of the researcher were to critically asses the sample size and distribution of the questionnaires in accordance with probability sampling frame.

As the first thing was to get permission from the organization and request letter from the school of psychology, the researcher did that and he got all the necessary permission qualification of the data collecting process.

Secondly, the researcher got a data frame from the organizations human resource department in crude basis. After that, the selection of participants of the study was done with a demanding procedures and the final decision was made. In this part, the researcher has selected two important data collection assistants with a clear orientation about the essentiality of the data for this research and how to assign each and every questionnaires for the diverse respondents of the study. This method has brought a fruitful result both from the respondents and data collectors.

Finally, the questionnaires were disseminated to the participants in March and returned within two weeks by the data collectors. And the total questionnaires returned out of 224 samples was 203. Moreover, the overall process of data collection was held in good spirit with the help and cooperation of the organization's employees and the data collectors in general. The response rate was also very much expected as the contingency of the data was enough. In doing so, the delivery of the data has capable to proceed with further process, especially for the demands of inferential statistics.

3.7 Scoring of Instruments

As in majority of attitudinal scales, all the instruments used here are computed with the arrangement of values in a continuum. To deal with that, all the scores of respondents in all the instruments be calculated in terms of the number of representation. That is literary means, when some respondents score very low in the instruments, it will be assumed as they have a low sense of OID, JI, OJ & OCB and in the dimension's within these variables.

Likewise, the interpretations of respondents' results get in to analyses by adding all the items in transforming each item by computing them to get an aggregate outputs. The dimensions within this study variables are also put into a distinct category to some purpose as well as a combined variable with their original instruments. On the other hand, the reversely coded items in the questionnaire were recorded while analyzing the final results.

In addition, the attitudinal scale which extends from (1= strongly disagree; 5=strongly agree) is working for all the instrument measurement patterns. To this end, the favorability of the respondents may vary, so that it will get into consideration that all the answers are equally valued as an honest response from the participants. The coding process of items was critically done to get an objective result which is free from bias from the researcher. In this regard, some items from different scales were reversely coded, these items are from job involvement scale item number 8 (to me, my job is only a small part of who I am.) Item number 13(Usually I feel detached from my job), from Procedural justice scale item number 23(I am not sure what determines how I can get a promotion in this organization), item number 25(It's not really possible to change things around me),item number 28(when changes are made in this organization, the employees usually lose out in the end).From OCB Sportsmanship dimension, item number 55(I consume a lot of time complaining about trivial matters),item number 56(I tend to make "mountains out of molehills), item number 57(I always focus on what's wrong rather than the positive side), item number 58(I always find fault with what the organization is doing),item number 59(I am the classic "squeaky wheel" that always needs greasing).

Generally, the scoring process of measurement results is the basis for this study that it is seen as an important aspect to get a valid and standardized outcome in the whole process of the research. Besides, the quality of the data in the result producing process is taking into account to assume an outstanding outcome from the computation of variables with different effects.

3.8 Data Analysis

In this study, the data are computed and analyzed using different statistical tools. In this regard, the description of statistical usages is classified into parts. The first part is primarily based on descriptive statistics that is measures of all the predictor (Organizational identification, Job involvement, organizational justice perceptions) and outcome variable (Organizational citizenship behavior) in relation to socio demographic characteristics of employees. Moreover, the second part is heavily an inferential statistic which is comprised of, MANOVA, (including Post Hoc analysis of significant scores), Pearson product moment correlation-test, Canonical correlation test and

Regression analysis are used and for values that were not qualified to meet with normality assumptions non - parametric tests used. In this regard, as APA (2010) clearly states, while testing different assumptions essential to the statistical model adopted (e.g. normality, homogeneity of variance, homogeneity of regression), and in model fitting must be checked seriously.

The next process was how the variables were computed in this study, first after the descriptive explanations of all the variables non parametric tests (Man Whitney &Wilcoxon Signed-ranks tests), MANOVA, and Regression analysis were applicable to socio-demographic characteristics of employees vs OCB, and including Pearson Product Moment correlation-test to see the impacts of predictor variables between OID vs OCB, JI vs OCB, DJ vs OCB, PJ vs OCB and IJ vs OCB aimed at calculating their relationships that includes the dimensions of OCB to specifically see the single and combined relationships with predictor variables. As in standardized research, the conditions of the data are tested for whether it has fulfilled the normality assumptions. (Which includes, skewness & kurtosis measure, Shapiro Wilk test with graph, Q-Q plots & box plots).

Furthermore, to observe the strong predictor variable and the amount of variance accounted for by independent variables to that of the dependent variable, Regression analysis and Canonical correlation were employed. In this context, to detect the strongest predictor of the OCB among (OID, JI, DJ, PJ, IJ). In this regard, the Stepwise regression analysis used to show the robustness predictor. In another way, canonical correlations were used to comprehend on OCB dimensions relationships with OID, JI, DJ, PJ, and IJ. Moreover, all the assumptions of the test are applied, including the multicollinearity of variables that may cause statistical adjustments. Besides, SPSS -23- statistical package is used to calculate research results in quantitative ways.

Generally, in this study while using statistical computations, all the necessary assumptions behind the tests were applied with thoughtful care and as to convince the credibility of the data analysis process through a scientific approach. It is also the researcher's responsibility to make sure that this investigation is worthwhile.

3.9 Data Quality Assurance
In all the process of this research, data quality is assured with different mechanisms, such as, the validity, reliability of the study as well as the relevance of the data in terms of the collection, presentation and recording. In this regard the psychometric properties of the data, including

instrumentation and measurement are held with quality. This particular research uses the standardized tools recommended by APA to research activities, regarding the sampling, interpretation of results in general and using data analysis specifically to determine whether the data is cleaned to proceed with further generalization. All the missing data are also being clearly reported to assure the unbiased notion of the data and other special effects.

The outputs of this research could serve as an indication to other related investigations with keeping the quality of results. In this case, the researcher was determined to be a critical as preserving the accuracy of the data and results. Moreover, the use of statistical operations in this research is going to be discussed with caution and understanding. The distribution of questionnaires to respondents was also delivered with neutrality in accessing the best quality data in order to be value free from the actual research results as possible as it could. Such measures for sure are believed to be important for guaranteeing the quality of the data at hand and the process of the research in wide-ranging.

Generally, data cleaning and the management of missing values has been critically observed in relation to the sort out of the data values precoding the missing values with system missing tabulation and other significant procedures to harmonize the quality of the data. In this regard, the respondents that are not capable of answering almost 75% of the items were not included in the final tabulation of the data. On the other hand, after all the respondents have given a total of 223 questionnaires the general return value was 202 which are fulfilled a minimum of data quality criterion that are attributed in doing strong data management formulations. This is occurring that, the 20 people were not returned due to many reasons and -1- respondent was returned the questionnaire but not fulfilling the minimum acceptance percentage rate. That is done with great care and the quality of the data has also been determined with the actual status of observed data in the current study. To substitute missing values linear interpolation technique which is replacing missing values using a linear interpolation of gender variance is used and this is done by last valid value before the missing value and the first valid value after the missing value are used for the interpolation. For all other variables series mean which replaces missing values with the mean for the entire series has been applied by using the SPSS software package.

3.10 Ethical Considerations

In this research conditions of ethical aspects are suspected in terms of having genuine data, which is not falsified or produced with care. As APA (2010) indicates scholarly researcher must emphasize on three important ethical and legal concerns; ensure the accuracy of scientific knowledge, protect the rights and welfare of research participants, and protect intellectual property rights (*p.* 11). This is the sole purpose of this research as tried to be following scientific methods of research.

According to the participants' protection, each and every respondent are getting voluntary partaking to the study. Mutual consent agreements provided for the involvement of respondents. In other words the process of this research is not communication with any deception, or other psychological methods that are not applicable in non-experimental researches.

The researcher facilitated necessary conditions to collect ethically sound data. For this to happen, all the process of the data collections is seriously taken. Respondents are told to be free to quit participating in the research any time they want, if there are any inconveniences with the contents or the procedures of this research. In this respect, the researcher is trying to be free from pushing the participants from joining in the research process in general.

Chapter Four

Results

4.1 Introduction

The major aim of this part is to make the analysis and interpretations of the investigated data. The chapter has been presented with different sections that are contextualized according to the objectives of the study and their dimension. The main characteristics of this chapter, moreover, is to give a comprehensive insight in accordance with the values and outcomes of study variables and with their technical tests. Furthermore, the chapter is organized with the following looks.

In the first section, the major parts of the analysis are, socio demographic characteristics of respondents and their descriptive values, the descriptive scores of the dependent variable and in relation to the socio demographic characteristics of the participants as well as the differences and relationships between the outcome variable and respondent characteristics in terms of their background. For its part, descriptive and inferential statistics with normality and non-normality assumptions used in different grounds. This section is particularly used to respond to the first objective of the study.

In the second section, the chief concern is to show the relationships among OID (Organizational Identification) and OCB (Organizational citizenship behaviors). In this regard, the descriptive scores of OID (Organizational identification) as one of the predictor variable will be provided in itself. Then, the next stage is to, make comparison across OI vs OCB by using statistical tests to substantiate the results in this portion. This part is organized to answer the second objective of the study

In the third section, the primary task is to compare JI (Job involvement) with OCB (Organizational citizenship Behavior), this is done by showing the relationships of the study variables. The descriptive results of JI by participants of the study is of course the initial step to be provided as to show the strength of the scores before further addressing advanced statistical tests. This is the realization of the third objective of the current study.

The fourth section is part of showing the relationship of OJ (perceived Organizational justice dimensions) and OCB (Organizational citizenship behavior) this is done by using the three dimensions, namely, DJ, (Distributive justice) PJ (Procedural justice) and IJ (Interactional justice)

with their effect on OCB independently and within the sub scales of OCB. Before that, the descriptive results of OJ's dimensions as a multidimensional scale will be presented. This section is heavily responding to the fourth objective of the current study.

The fifth section of this chapter is focusing on the interaction of an OID (Organizational identification), JI (Job involvement), DJ (Distributive justice), PJ(Procedural justice) and IJ(Interactional justice) to that of OCB (Organizational citizenship behavior). In this part advanced tests that show interactions as well as predictions are used heavily.

In general, this chapter is more of quantitative applicability of deduced facts and was part of the systematic presentation of the study variables in accordance with their numeric interpretation. All the way, the strict assumptions of statistical tests were applied as part and parcel of the power and robustness of the study findings and the generalization that are attributed from the results. In doing so, different tests will be used. And as it is good to know that abbreviations of study variables were used in most parts as the indicators of the study variables. These are OID (Organizational identification), JI (Job involvement), OJ (Organizational justice), DJ (distributive justice), PJ (Procedural justice), IJ (Interactional justice), and OCB (Organizational Citizenship behavior) that are used interchangeably in different parts of the chapter.

4.2 Socio- Demographic Characteristics of the study participants

In the current study, there were different qualities observed from participants, as their backgrounds are differed due to different reasons, there also are shared features with different contexts. In addition, the diverse population in the organization has also been the factor behind different qualities of the participants in order to have varied appearances. Moreover, in this study there were 202 sample participants that were eligible for analysis of the results. The socio demographic characteristics of the participants were bounded by major factors as, gender, Age, Work experience, Educational status and Income. This is presented with detailed description afterwards by the next table.

Table-3- The background characteristics of study participants (N=202)

Socio demographic Characteristics	Label	Frequency	Percentage (%)
Gender	Male	94	46.5
	Female	108	53.5
	18-29	49	24.3
Age	30-40	92	45.5
	41-50	43	21.3
	≥ 51	18	8.9
	0-5	36	17.8
Work	6-10	54	26.7
experience	11-15	35	17.3
(In years)	16-20	14	6.9
	21-25	16	7.9
	26-30	21	10.4
	≥31	26	12.9
	Preparatory & Below	40	19.8
Educational	Vocational & Diploma	63	31.2
background	Undergraduate	72	35.6
	Post Graduate	27	13.6
	500- 1500	33	16.3
Income	1501-2500	25	12.4
(In Birr)	2501-3500	22	10.9
	3501-4500	39	19.3
	4501-5500	21	10.4
	5501-6500	15	7.4
	>6501	47	23.3

As it is indicated in table -3- there were different characteristics of study participants, from the total, 202 participants of the study, 98 (46.5%) were males and 108 (53.5%) were females. In this regard females were greater in number than male participants. In relation to age groups of the participants, from 18-29 (24.3%, n=49), from 30-40 (45.5%, n=92), from 41-50 (21.3%, n=43), and ≥ 51 there were (8.9, n=18) participants accordingly. Concerning, to work experience the study participants who were experienced from 0-5 years are (17.8%, n =36), from 6-10 years of experience there were (26.7%, n=54) participants, from 11-15 years there were (17.3%, n=35), from 16-20 years there were (6.9%, n=14) participants and from 21-25 years of experience there were (7.9%, n=16) participants as well as from 26- 30 there are (10.4%, n=21) and finally from 31 and above years of work experience there were (12.9%, n= 26) participants. In relation to educational status of the study participants, there have been (19.8%, n=40) who were an academic status with preparatory and below grade levels, (31.2%, n=63) were having vocational & diploma level of education and the rest (35.6%, n=72) were having an undergraduate degree as well as (13.4%, n=27) were post graduates. As the Income of the participants were also computed there has been differences between them. (16.3%, n=33) were getting 1000-1500 Birr per- month, (12.4%, n=25) were also getting 1501-2500 Birr per month, (10.9%, n=22) were getting 2501-3500 Birr per month, (19.3%, n=39) were getting between 3501-4500 Birr per month, (10.4%, n=21) were getting 4501-550 Birr per month, (7.4%, n=15) were getting 5501-6500 Birr per month and the rest (23.3%, n=47) were part of the study participants who have earned above and equals to 6501 Ethiopian Birr.

4.2.1 Socio - Demographic variable and OCB

As part of assessing the context of OCB in relation to socio demographic characteristics of this particular study is one of the major purpose of this study. In is basics, OCB has been associated with different predictor variables as to notice the best and more related ones in order to see organizational effectiveness in both in role and the extra role behavioral patterns. Thus, OCB could be Interpreted using its Five Dimensions (Altruism, Conscientiousness, Sportsmanship, Courtesy, Civic virtue) his dimensions are used to show the detail parts of OCB. Moreover OCB is also as a unidimensional scale which can be interpreted with its overall items. Furthermore the scores of OCB and its dimensions are provided below.

Table-4- Results of descriptive statistics of study participants overall OCB and its dimensions

Outcome variable	N	Items	Min	Max	Mean	SD
Overall OCB	202	24	44.00	116.00	93.79	12.21
Altruism	202	5	5.00	25.00	19.88	3.51
Conscientiousness	202	5	5.00	25.00	20.21	3.49
Sportsmanship	202	5	5.00	21.00	9.78	4.07
Courtesy	202	5	5.00	25.00	19.00	4.13
Civic-virtue	202	4	4.00	20.00	14.83	3.16

As presented in table- 4- study participants scored a relatively high in general with the overall OCB total (M=93.79, SD = 12.22). Which is above the expected level of the general mean score of (24*5=120) total highest hypothetical result from the five point Likert scale. As these scores generally shows, there is an optimist line of behaving OCB among participants of the study at least in its simplest level. Other than that, from the sub dimensions, Altruism has been scored (M =19.89, SD=3.52) out of its five total items in the Likert scale from which (5*5=25). This is also an indication of the fact that there is a slightly better sense of altruistic parts of OCB among participants of the study in general. In accordance with conscientiousness dimension participants were also be scored a decent result (M=20.21, SD=3.49) from the total highest expected score of (5*5=25) in its five items. . On the other, Sportsmanship dimension of OCB has the lowest results so far from the participants (M=9.78, SD=4.1) as it is below the average of (5*5=25) highest value of the five items within this sub dimension. From that, one can literary realized that the current study participants showed a very little citizen-like postures in relationships with others in their organization. Courtesy is also one of the major dimensions of OCB and in this particular study the respondents has been scored (M=19.01, SD=4.14) as it is reasonable score. This dimension has been measured by five items which take after, (5*5=25) expected highest score. Finally, civic virtue was also being examined as part of OCB dimensions and participants of the study gained (M=14.83, SD=3.16) from the total of (4*5=20) expected highest score. This is labeled as a good score of actual and active political participations of employees in the internal organizational context.

Table -5-The results of descriptive statistics showing OCB and Socio demographic variables

Outcome variable	Predictor Variables		N	Mean	SD	SE
	Gender	Male	94	93.65	12.24	1.26
		Female	108	93.92	12.25	1.18
	Age	18-29	49	94.99	10.30	1.47
		30-40	92	91.81	13.99	1.46
		41-50	43	96.17	9.95	1.52
Overall		≥51	18	96.64	8.02	1.89
OCB	Work experience	0-5	36	92.23	12.37	2.06
	(In years)	6-10	54	92.37	13.96	1.90
		11-15	35	91.06	13.96	2.36
		16-20	14	97.74	7.87	2.10
		21-25	16	96.35	10.44	2.61
		26-30	21	97.30	11.19	2.44
		≥ 31	26	96.08	7.86	1.54
		Preparatory & Below	40	94.60	13.98	2.21
		Vocational & Diploma	63	91.28	13.34	1.68
		Undergraduate	72	96.29	9.292	1.09
	Educational	Post Graduate	27	92.90	11.25	2.17
	Background	500-1500	33	92.17	13.99	2.44
		1501-2500	25	93.98	9.74	1.95
		2501-3500	22	91.43	11.16	2.38
	Income	3501-4500	39	92.40	14.21	2.27
	(In Birr)	4501-5500	21	95.31	13.59	2.96
		5501-6500	15	96.59	9.22	2.38
		≥6501	47	95.52	11.12	1.62

As table -5- demonstrates the overall results of OCB in relation to the study participants' characteristics was computed and the subsequent results were found in general. Male and female participants were not that much differed in their overall OCB scores. As they have scored relatively same results. On the other hand, all age groups also scored good OCB in general, the work experience, educational background, income levels are not much differed between the scores of overall OCB. But to make sure that this scores are statistically significant indifference or not further tests were computed in next parts. Because it is not possible to only justify statistical results based on their descriptive results. In this regard, the potential of study participants' socio-demographic characteristics in order to show some variation or relationships has to be taken into account for actual verification and quality results. The tendency of getting high scores in the outcome variable has also been subject to different factors, including the influences that are brought by the predictor variables of the current study.

4.2.2 Gender and OCB

According to the current studies objectives socio- demographic variables had been taken as one of the hypothesized predictors of OCB. Then, from the suggested variables gender is the primary one. In doing so basically associational statistical computations and differences across gender groups were delivered. In general, before deciding on what is the best statistical test presentation of the level of the data's normality and related presuppositions have been applied. Because of that, the applicable level of tests for this variable in relation to OCB was a non-parametric tests.

Table -6- Mann- Whitney and Wilcoxon test results by gender and OCB (N=202)

	Overall OCB	Altruism	Conscientiousness	Sportsmanship	Courtesy	Civic –virtue
Mann Whitney	4756.000	4533.500	4728.00	4307.500	4460.000	4712.000
U	8942.000	8719.500	8914.000	9872.500	10025.00	8898.000
Wilcoxon W	-.054	-.623	-.126	-1.203	-.806	-.167
z	.957	.534	.900	.229	.420	.867
Sig. (2-tailed)						

a. Grouping Variable: Gender

According to the non–parametric test results above in table-6- Mann-Whitney test indicated that there is no difference between Male (*Mdn* = 93.79) employees overall OCB scores and females (*Mdn*= 93.79), $U=4756$, $p=.957$, $r=-.03$ which means their participation on extra role behaviors is almost the same and there are no difference among the participant gender and their level of behaving in the dimensions of OCB. For instance, there is no difference on altruism among Male (*Mdn*=20) and Female (*Mdn*=20), $U=4533.50$, $p=.53$, $r=-.04$. In relation to conscientiousness there is also no difference between males (*Mdn*=20) and females (*Mdn*=20.21), $U=4728$, $p=.90$, $r = -.0.01$. In other hands, sportsmanship scores were also no difference between males (*Mdn*=10) and females (*Mdn*=9.89), *U*=4307.50, *p*=.229 *r* =-.08. Courtesy has no difference between male (*Mdn*=4460), *p*=.450, *r* =-.06. Finally the scores of civic- virtue is not also differed between male (*Mdn*=15) and females (*Mdn*=15), *p*=.87, *r*= -0.01.

It is also true that the test scores of Wilcoxon signed rank test has also showed that clearly indicated that there is no difference between the overall OCB scores of male and female respondents and its dimension, for instance, in overall OCB male(*Mdn*= 93.79) and Females(*Mdn* =93.79),z = -.05, *p* =.957, *r* = -.03.

In general, as the tests above critically showed that there were no difference between SHOPR study participant employees 'on both the overall OCB and its specific dimensions. That is to say, this is the fact that only address gender groups and their attributes. From this instance, it can be deduced that there is very good organizational citizenship behavior pattern among male and female employees of SHOPR, which was without significance difference between the two groups based on their median and ranks of scores.

4.2.3 Age and OCB

As one of the determinant socio -demographic variables in the current study, age groups of employees were computed to get the actual statistical results. In this regard the appropriate test was multiple analysis of variance (MANOVA) test that could be determined the variabilities of independent groups on the dependent variables.

Table-7-Multivariate Test results of Overall OCB & its dimensions across different Age groups of participants(N=202)

Effect		Value	F	Hypothesis df	Error df	Sig.
Intercept	Pillai's Trace	.991	3541.053[b]	6.000	193.000	.000
	Wilks' Lambda	.009	3541.053[b]	6.000	193.000	.000
	Hotelling's Trace	110.085	3541.053[b]	6.000	193.000	.000
	Roy's Largest Root	110.085	3541.053[b]	6.000	193.000	.000
Age	Pillai's Trace	.100	1.124	18.000	585.000	.323
	Wilks' Lambda	.902	1.123	18.000	546.372	.325
	Hotelling's Trace	.105	1.120	18.000	575.000	.327
	Roy's Largest Root	.057	1.837[c]	6.000	195.000	.094

a. Design: Intercept + Age
b. Exact statistic
c. The statistic is an upper bound on F that yields a lower bound on the significance level.

As table -7- showed, there was no statistically significant difference among participants OCB levels based on their age groups, $F(18,546)=1.123$, $p=.325$; Wilk's $\lambda=0.902$. Generally, the multiple comparison of variables indicated that there was no significant difference between the age groups of SHOPR employees with respect to their overall OCB results, $F(3,198) = 1.911$, $p=.121$. That means, the OCB scores of 18-29 years of age ($M=94.98$, $SD=10.30$) has no difference from age groups 30-40 ($M=91.49$, $SD=14.34$); 41-50 ($M=96.12$, $SD=9.96$); ≥ 51($M=96.6442$, $SD=8.02$). And there is no need to see the variations of the age groups with post hoc analysis. In addition, employees of SHOPR were not significantly different with their OCB dimension scores except Altruism. From the results, Altruism scores of respondents significantly varied by their age groups, F (3,198) =2.843, $p=$. 039. However, A Tukey post hoc test showed no significant difference among age groups which indicated that there were only a slight variation between each other's age group. On the other hand, there was no significant difference between the age groups and their responses on the Conscientiousness dimension of OCB, F (3,198) =2.302, $p=$.078. There was also no significant difference between age groups and their Sportsmanship scores, F (3,198) = .966, $p=$.410. Moreover, there was no significant difference between age groups Courtesy level, F (3,198) =1.637, p =.182. It is also held true that there is no significant difference among the participants age groups and there Civic-virtue patterns, F (3,198) = 1.017, $p=$.386.

4.2.4 Work Experience and OCB

Work experience was one of the fundamental variables which hypothesized to be affected the overall all and dimensions of OCB. In this regard, the assumptions of normality before the actual application of the tests were employed. This is to make sure whether there are violations against the normality concerns.

Table-8-Multivariate Test results of Overall OCB & its dimensions across different Work experience of participants(N=202)

Effect		Value	F	Hypothesis df	Error df	Sig.
Intercept	Pillai's Trace	.992	3976.829[b]	6.000	190.000	.000
	Wilks' Lambda	.008	3976.829[b]	6.000	190.000	.000
	Hotelling's Trace	125.584	3976.829[b]	6.000	190.000	.000
	Roy's Largest Root	125.584	3976.829[b]	6.000	190.000	.000
Experience	Pillai's Trace	.153	.852	36.000	1170.000	.718
	Wilks' Lambda	.855	.846	36.000	837.109	.726
	Hotelling's Trace	.161	.842	36.000	1130.000	.734
	Roy's Largest Root	.063	2.058[c]	6.000	195.000	.060

a. Design: Intercept + Experience

b. Exact statistic

c. The statistic is an upper bound on F that yields a lower bound on the significance level.

As it is shown in the table, there was no statistically significant difference among participants OCB levels based on their work experience, F (36,817) =.817, p=.726; Wilk's λ=.855. It is also true that as multiple comparison of variables portrayed, there are no significant difference between work experience and overall OCB scores of SHOPR employees, F (6,195) = 1.207, p =.304. In this respect, it is clear that in the actual context the SHOPR workers have no variations in their overall OCB levels across different work experiences. In this regard, the overall mean scores across different work experience categories were not much alike and it tends to good OCB level. Employees with 0-5 years of experience have (M=92.24, SD=12.38),employees with 6-10 years of experience have (M=92.37, SD=13.96), employees with 11-15 years of experience have (M=91.06, SD=13.96), employees with 16-20 years of experience have (M=97.74, SD=7.87), employees with 21-25 years of experience have (M=96.35, SD=10.44), employees with 26-30 years of experience have (M=97.30, SD=11.19) and employees with $\geq$ 31 years of experience have (M=96.08, SD= 7.86) of OCB results. In this regard, work experience did not much with employees OCB patterns, especially in relation to its dimensions, Altruism, F(6,195)=1.157, p =.331; Conscientiousness,F(6,195)=0.995,p=.430;Sportmanship$F$(6,195)=0.73,p=63;Courtesy,F(6,195= 1.170, p =.324; Civic-virtue F (6,195)=1.465 p=.192. This an indication that work experience does not cause variation in the dimensions of OCB in SHOPR employees. Generally speaking, SHOPR employees have a very good level OCB dimensions, but there is no difference between their work experiences in order to behave in extra role behavioral patterns.

4.2.5 Educational Status and OCB

Educational level may also be one of the most contributory factors in providing to OCB and its dimensions. To proceed on that, the preliminary assumptions of normality were facilitated and the results showed that there is an acceptable level of normality to deal with robust statistical tests.

Table-9-Multivariate Test results of Overall OCB & its dimensions across different Educational status of participants(N=202)

Effect		Value	F	Hypothesis df	Error df	Sig.
Intercept	Pillai's Trace	.992	4217.246[b]	6.000	193.000	.000
	Wilks' Lambda	.008	4217.246[b]	6.000	193.000	.000
	Hotelling's Trace	131.106	4217.246[b]	6.000	193.000	.000
	Roy's Largest Root	131.106	4217.246[b]	6.000	193.000	.000
Education	Pillai's Trace	.089	.992	18.000	585.000	.467
	Wilks' Lambda	.913	.990	18.000	546.372	.469
	Hotelling's Trace	.093	.988	18.000	575.000	.471
	Roy's Largest Root	.060	1.963[c]	6.000	195.000	.073

a. Design: Intercept + Education

b. Exact statistic

c. The statistic is an upper bound on F that yields a lower bound on the significance   level.

As it is shown above, there was no statistically significant difference among participants OCB levels based on their educational status, $F(18,546) = .990$, $p=.469$; Wilk's $\lambda=.913$. This is an indication that all the mean values of respondents by educational status has not varied accordingly. Even if the participants of the study had a slightly higher level of OCB, as multiple comparison results revealed, participants were not differed in their overall OCB by their educational levels $F(47,154) = 2.098$, $p=.102$. Moreover, OCB dimensions had not been significantly differed by respondents' educational status, excluding the case of conscientiousness. In this regard, the all the five dimensions of OCB have been recorded different means by the educational levels of participants. Especially there were less scores in sportsmanship dimension as it was observed from the respondents. In general, Conscientiousness has, F (7,194) = 2.886, p =.037, participants of the study were significantly differed by their educational status. A Tukey post hoc test revealed that the results of vocational & diploma holders (M=19.41, SD=3.60) was significantly differed with employees at undergraduate level (M=21.10, SD=2.76).Sportsmanship has, F= (7,194) =.963, p=.411; Courtesy has, F (7,194) = 1.955, p=.122; Civic-virtue has, F (7,194) =.979, p=.403.

4.2.6 Income and OCB

In the process of preparing for normality tests of participant's income in relation and their OCB level. In this particular category, the skewness and kurtosis level are normal, but some of them are kurtosis data that do not fall under the normality assumption. After this has been done, the researcher decided to continue with the tests that needs normality assumptions. Because most of the graphs and the actual statistical outputs of skewness and kurtosis has shown that one can proceed with cautious.

Table-10-Multivariate Test results of Overall OCB & its dimensions across different Incomes of participants(N=202)

Effect		Value	F	Hypothesis df	Error df	Sig.
Intercept	Pillai's Trace	.993	4278.993[b]	6.000	190.000	.000
	Wilks' Lambda	.007	4278.993[b]	6.000	190.000	.000
	Hotelling's Trace	135.126	4278.993[b]	6.000	190.000	.000
	Roy's Largest Root	135.126	4278.993[b]	6.000	190.000	.000
Income	Pillai's Trace	.204	1.144	36.000	1170.000	.258
	Wilks' Lambda	.809	1.149	36.000	837.109	.254
	Hotelling's Trace	.220	1.151	36.000	1130.000	.250
	Roy's Largest Root	.113	3.672[c]	6.000	195.000	.002

a. Design: Intercept + Income

b. Exact statistic

c. The statistic is an upper bound on F that yields a lower bound on the significance level.

As the table has discussed above there was no significant difference between participants OCB levels and their monthly income, F (36,837) = 1.149, p=.254; Wilk's λ=.809. It was also proved by multiple comparison results. As the participants mean scores on overall OCB resembles to the highest level, they were not varied amongst their monthly income. This is expressed as, F (6,195) = 0.557, p=.764 .In this regard, all the respondents have been resembles to the highest level of OCB. That needs to be a great implication of the actual conditions of SHOPR employees in relation to their OCB level and the income they earn from the organization which has no significant variation in terms of behaving to take extra role activities in context. The OCB dimensions were also not differentiated by the income levels of participants of the study. In this regard, all the five dimensions are fulfilled with the same characteristics across income categories of individuals within the situation of each dimensions mean values. However the mean scores of sportsmanship dimension have been much less than the other dimensions mean values, all other dimensions have near results which are likely to be taken as high in the dimension scores as, F(6,195)=1.028, p=.408 in Civic-virtue; F (6,195) =1.395, p=.218, in Consciousness, F (6,195)=1.837, p=.904 in Sportsmanship F (6,195) =.458, p=.839 in Courtesy and, F (6,195) =.917, p= .484. In this regard, it is clear that there is no variation among participants of the study in OCB's dimensions.

4.2.7 Overall Prediction of Socio-Demographic Variables with OCB

This is last part where the socio-demographic variables were critically assessed whether they are fit to predict OCB in general. To deal with this, all the possible preconditions that are presupposing to multiple linear regression assumptions were fully analyzed.

Table-11- Multiple Regression analysis of Overall OCB and Socio demographic variables (202)

Model	Unstandardized Coefficients		Standardized Coefficients	t	Sig.
	B	Std. Error	Beta		
(Constant)	89.208	4.597		19.405	.000
Gender	.915	1.778	.038	.514	.607
Age	-1.134	1.279	-.084	-.886	.376
Experience	1.114	.548	.190	2.033	.043
Education	-.194	1.215	-.015	-.160	.873
Income	.588	.576	.105	1.022	.308

a. Dependent Variable: Overall OCB

As table -11- showed, there was no significant overall predictors of OCB from the socio demographic variables and their categories in particular. This is determined by ANOVA results prior to the actual regression outputs as $F (201) = 1.391$, $p=.229$. Which clearly showed that the contribution of socio-demographic variables to predict Overall OCB is not significant. Because the share of contribution that is due to socio demographic factors is only accounted for, 3.6% to forecast OCB. In other words Overall OCB has not been affected by such variables for instance overall OCB and gender has , $\beta=.915$, $t(201)=.514$, $p=.607$, Overall OCB and Age has, $\beta=-1.134$, $t(201)= -.886$, $p=.376$, overall OCB and Work experience has, $\beta=1.114$, $t(201)= 2.033$, $P=0.43$, this shows work experience has few predicting power of overall OCB, Education has $\beta= -.194$, $t (201)= -.160$, $p=.873$ and Income has $\beta=.588$, $t(201)=1.022$, $p=.308$. The total predicted amount of this variables is, $R^2=.034$.

Table-12- General explanation of each OCB dimensions by Model summary and ANOVA

OCB Dimensions	R	R Square	Adjusted R Square	Std. Error of the Estimate	df	F	Sig.
Altruism	.161[a]	.026	.001	3.51777	5	1.048	.391[b]
Conscientiousness	·225[a]	.051	.026	3.44607	5	2.087	.069[b]
Sportsmanship	.182[a]	.033	.008	4.05366	5	1.343	.248[b]
Courtesy	.159[a]	.025	.000	4.13543	5	1.068	.408[b]
Civic Virtue	.105[a]	.011	-.014	3.18475	5	.447	.822[b]

a. Predictors: (Constant), Gender, Age, Experience, Education, Income

b. As the results indicated, each dimension was calculated in separate tables and put like this to comprehend

As the above table indicated, the dimensions of OCB have not been significantly predicted by socio- demographic variables. For instance, altruism has been 2.6% of the total outcome was attributed from socio demographic variables, in relation to conscientious there are also 5.1% of the overall effect is explained from Socio demographic variable. Sportsmanship dimension has 3.3% proportion of explanation which is directly associated with socio – demographic variables, Courtesy has also been 2.5% of the share which is explained by Socio demographic variables, civic- virtue has 1.1% of which is explained from socio - demographic variables.

In general, Organizational citizenship behavior (OCB) is minimally related to Participants Socio-demographic characteristics. It has also been indicated in different computations held in this section as there are no significant differences between Gender, Age, Work Experience, Educational qualification and monthly income of employees of (SHOPR) in terms of overall OCB results and Its dimensions.

From these results, one can deduce that there is no significant relationship between OCB and socio demographic variables specifically in the study area. However, the overall OCB score of the participants is very good as the ($M=93.78, SD=12.22$) from the total expected results of 120 maximum OCB value from the 24 items in Likert scale. This is impressive to have in public organizations nowadays because of different factors that are responsible to contribute to lack of such extra role activities. On the other hand, the dimensions of OCB have also been

assessed with detailed analysis and participants of the study were not differed in their socio -
demographic background and their reaction to the five dimensions. There are also scores high
in these dimensions in most cases, but the participants' Sportsmanship ability has been found
low as the total output indicated. To critically observe Sportsmanship mean and standard
deviation scores in relation to socio demographic variables (M=9.78, SD= 4.01) was observed
in this dimension which is below the total expected value of 25 as five items in Likert scale.
The other dimensions like altruism has (M=19.88, SD=3.52) in relation to socio demographic
characteristics from the 5 items Likert scale and out of 25 highest possible scores.
Conscientiousness has (M=20.21, SD=3.49), from the five items that was measured by 5 items
Likert scale with 25 highest values. Courtesy has also been observed in relation to the mean and
standard deviation (M=19.02, SD = 4.14), as it was measured in the five items Likert scale.
Civic virtue also was the fifth dimension of OCB and the participants scored (M=14.836,
SD=3.16),out of the total four items and a maximum expected highest score is 20 As it was
observed participants of the study were having good OCB level and they are not differed by
their socio- demographic characteristics.

4.3 Employees Organizational Identification, Job Involvement, Perceived Organizational Justice and OCB

In the current research, organizational identification, Job involvement and perceived Organizational justice dimensions were among the predictor variables that could contribute to the presence of OCB.

Table-13-Results of descriptive statistics of study participants on overall Organizational Identification, Job Involvement, Organizational Justice dimensions and OCB (202)

	N	Minimum	Maximum	Mean	SD
Organizational identification	202	6.00	30.00	23.58	4.31
Job involvement	202	17.00	50.00	36.71	5.53
Distributive Justice	202	6	30	16.07	5.892
Procedural Justice	202	21	61	41.48	7.26
Interactional Justice	202	9	45	29.20	7.89
Overall OCB	202	44	116	93.79	12.22
Altruism	202	5.00	25.00	19.88	3.52
Conscientiousness	202	5.00	25.00	20.21	3.49
Sportsmanship	202	5.00	21.00	9.79	4.07
Courtesy	202	5.00	25.00	19.00	4.13
Civic virtue	202	4.00	20.00	14.83	3.16

As table-13 shown, Organizational identification was computed and the mean and standard deviation of scores ($M=23.57$, $SD=4.31$) is considered to be high in terms of the actual expected value of $6*5 =30$ total scores. Because, in this research the higher the scores are treated to be higher in the participants tendencies. This is going to be analyzed well in the next sections and there are different comparisons with the composition of Organizational identification in relation to the actual performance of participants.

Moreover, participants Job involvement has been measured with 1-5 Likert scale and from the 10 total items ($M =36.71$, $SD = 5.53$) was calculated and then it could be considered as a good score from the research participants. In this regard, one must be so curious that the variations in participants in overall OCB were too high than that of Job involvement ($M=93.79$, $SD=5.53$). The final scores of this group can further be interpreted with other statistical details and the effect it brought to the relationships of the predictor and outcome variables. In sum, Participants were scored a minimum of 17 and a maximum of 50 from the total of (5*10=50) expected scores in the continuum.

Furthermore, there was a description of organizational justice variables and its comparison with overall OCB and its dimensions. For instance, from the total 6 items of Distributive justice the minimum score was 6 and the maximum was 30 which was calculated from the total of (6*5=30), and (M=16.07, SD=5.892), which was in the middle from total scores. On the other hand Procedural justice was composed of 13 items and the minimum score of 21 and the maximum score was 61 out of the total(5*13=65), and (M=41.48, SD=7.263) that it indicted a good character across the participants conception of justice in this specific dimension. Likewise, Interactional justice scores had been also been calculated and the minimum of 9 and the maximum of 45 points (M = 29.20, SD=7.899) *were* scored out of the total 9 items which was calculated from (5*13=45) expected points. This is somehow above the half of the total score that was hypothetically crossed under the normal condition.

4.3 The Relationships among Organizational Identification, Job Involvement, perceived Organizational Justice and OCB

After all the necessary steps that are fully realized assumptions of correlational tests, like variable measurement type, the linearity of relationships between variables, whether there are outliers or not and normality of data distribution. The OID, JI, DJ, PJ, IJ and OCB variables were not found to violate many of such assumptions and the possible tests of relationships were applied in order to critically observe the constructs associations.

Table-14-The Relationships of Organizational identification, Job Involvement, Distributive justice , Procedural Justice and Interactional justice with OCB(202)

	Overall OCB	Altruism	Conscientiousness	Sportsmanship	Courtesy	Civic virtue
OID	.285**	.325**	.332**	-.016	.143*	.240**
Sig. (2-tailed)	.000	.000	.000	.817	.042	.001
JI	.392**	.355**	.378**	-.157*	.289**	.302**
Sig. (2-tailed)	.000	.000	.000	.026	.000	.000
DJ	.123	.170*.	.145*	.046	.088	127
Sig. (2-tailed)	.068	016	.040	.512	.215	.073
PJ	295**	.309**	.288**	.022	.177*	.271**
Sig. (2-tailed)	.000	.000	.000	.758	.012	.000
IJ	.322**	.336**	.304**	-.061	.242**	.241**
Sig. (2-tailed)	.000	.000	.000	.386	.001	.001

**. Correlation is significant at the 0.01 level (2-tailed).

*. Correlation is significant at the 0.05 level (2-tailed).

In the above table the correlation result has shown that there was a statistically significant, positive, but weak relationship between organizational identification and overall Organizational citizenship behavior of participants of the study, as r (200) =.285, $p < .01$ This is an indication of the fact that the highest level of organizational identification of participants of the study would somehow leads to high OCB level in general. But there is no causal relationship between these two variables as there are various extraneous and confounding variables that could affect the relationships of the variables. Organizational identification values of participants of the study have also been calculated in order to see its association with OCB's dimensions. By this, the results showed that OID was having a positive relationship with Altruism, r (200) =.325, p<.001, which is moderate in terms of strength, Organizational identification also has been positively correlated with conscientiousness, r(200)=.332, p<.01. It is clearly indicated that there is a significant but moderate relationship between the two variables concerning the strength the relationship. On the other hand, Organizational identification was inversely correlated with Sportsmanship dimension, but the association is not significant which is not implicated whether the one's score affects the other part, r (200) = -.016, p =.817. OID was also related to Courtesy in the positive direction and the strength of the relationship is somehow weak r (200) =.143, p=.043. Finally, organizational identification was also positively associated with the civic- virtue of participants of the study, r (200) =.240, p=.001. In general, the Organizational identification has a positive relationship with four of the dimensions of OCB. This is also true that the combination of these variables is somehow related to Organizational identification.

On the other hand, participants Job involvement was positively correlated with their Overall OCB. The relationship was significant and somehow weak in linearity, r(200) =.391, p<.001. Which was considered as the possibility of Job involvement to have some effect in participants overall OCB. From the results it is possible to have some clue that job involvement and Overall OCB have statistically related in accordance with the current research participants. Job involvement has also been significant relationships with OCB dimensions. These relationships have been expressed with different instances. For instance, weak Job involvement and Altruism had positive, highly significant and weak in the linearity of the relationships (200) =.355, p<.001. The correlation between Job involvement and Conscientiousness dimension was also significant, positive and somehow weak in linearity, r (200), =.378, p<.001. On the other hand Sportsmanship and Job involvement had also been inversely correlated as, r (200) = -.157, p=.026. This was an indication that job involvement and sportsmanship has no mutual and positive relationships that the increment in one variable may not influence the same effect in the other variable. It is also possible to deduce that employees were having good job involvement levels in the absence of showing extra role behaviors that are related with others by tolerating the inconveniences in day today life and even they may decline to tolerate their colleagues. Job involvement had also been correlated with Courtesy dimensions of OCB, r (200) =.289, $p<.001$, the relationship was highly significant, positive and weak in linearity. Civic-virtue dimension of OCB, was also correlated with Job involvement, which was highly significant, positive and weak in linearity, r (200) =.302, $p<.001$.

From the above explanations Job involvement had significantly correlated with all the five dimensions of OCB but in different directions. This showed that job involvement is indeed related to OCB dimensions within the context of the current study participants of SHOPR employees. In sum, there was a tendency that the employees OCB level was also associated with their Job involvement patterns in the organization. It is also an important factor in the current research that it assumed that Job involvement was taken as one of predictor variables to affect employees OCB. It clearly showed that Job involvement could be stand in to this reality, because in the current research it was proved that job involvement is associated with OCB and its dimensions. In this regard, SHOPR employees who were highly anticipated to their job involvement could also be getting higher participation in overall OCB and most of its dimensions. Moreover, job involvement had been investigated in detail whether it was considered as the predictor variable for OCB. The research findings supported this notion and it was clearly indicated that job involvement could determine the employees OCB occurrence as well as the dimensions of this variable.

Moreover, perceived Organizational justice is also one of the predictor variables that could contribute to the occurrences of OCB in general. This is due to different reasons that have possibly determined the values of OJ in organizational contexts. As there are dimensions of OJ are further discussed in distributive, Procedural and interactional patterns, the relationship between these dimensions and the existence of OCB must be observed in the current research context. In this regard, there was no significant relationship between Distributive justice perceptions of participants and there over all OCB scores. This is an indication that the SHOPR employees was not behaving in OCB patterns because of the belief in their organization's tendency to have fairness in the allocation of resources in response to the responsibility of employees, $r(200)=.123$, $p=.068$. This could be interpreted in different ways, for instance, employees was considerate of achieving OCB patterns without the existence of possible fairness in organizational resource allocation and etc. Distributive justice perceptions had been been significantly associated, Altruism, r (200) =.170, p =.016, which was a positive, and weak in the linearity of relationships. On the other hand Distributive justice also had related to Conscientiousness dimensions of OCB, r (200) =.145, p =.040. From this regard, one can conclude that Distributive justice perceptions of employees of SHOPR was proved to be related with two of the five dimensions of OCB, but this relationship is   weak in linearity. These relationships could be explained by employees distributive justice perceptions may help with a little bit of altruism and the conscientiousness pattern of their day to day life.

Furthermore, employees procedural justice perceptions was indeed strongly correlated with overall OCB, the relationship was significant, positive and weak in linearity r (200) =.29, p<.001. From this instance, it can be deduced that SHOPR employees' Procedural justice perception was believed to contribute to the availability of overall OCB and this was not taken as a causal effect however. Procedural justice perceptions of employees were also compared against OCB dimensions and of course there was a significant relationship with most of the dimensions. For instance, Altruism had significantly related to Procedural justice, r (202) =.309, p<.001 and the relationship was positive as well as weak in linearity. Conscientiousness was also been significantly related to Procedural justice perceptions of SHOPR employees, r (200) =.288, p<.001. The relationship was positive, and weak in linearity however. The difference in this regard was observed from Sportsmanship, which was not significantly related to Procedural justice perceptions of employees, r (200) =.022 p=.758, this is an indication that the process of fairness in decision making had nothing to do with employees' ability to show citizen-like posture in relationships with others by tolerating the inconveniences that are predictable and accept burdens of work without complaints. Courtesy has been also had significant relationship with Procedural justice perceptions of employees with positive direction and weak in linearity (200) =.177, p=.012. Finally, civic virtue of employees was also significantly related to Procedural justice perceptions, r (200) =.271, p<.001. This relationship was quite positive, but weak in linearity. In general, there was a probability that Procedural justice perceptions of employees were correlated with OCB four out of the five OCB dimensions and the relationship is somehow showed the contribution of procedural justice as to contribute to the occurrences of OCB dimensions in SHOPR. The logical inference from this case could be taken. There are more or less characteristic of the variables that interplays each other to have some effect on employees organizational behavioral patterns, especially in terms of having an extra role and voluntary activities within the organization.

Finally, Interactional justice concerned with how the employees' perception regarding whether their thoughts and needs are considered through making job decisions in an organization. This construct is proposed as one of the predictor variables that are possibly bestowed to the availability of OCB. Respecting that, Interactional justice perception of employees in SHOPR was correlated with most of OCB dimensions. For instance, Interactional justice perception is correlated with Altruism dimensions of OCB with positive and weak in linearity of the relationship, $(200) = .336$, $p < .001$ .Interactional justice is also highly correlated with Conscientiousness dimension of OCB, with positive direction and weak in the linearity of relationship $(200) = .304$, $p = .001$. On the other hand Sportsmanship dimension of OCB had not been found correlated with interactional justice perceptions of employees, $r (200) = -.061$, $p = .386$. Sportsmanship charcteristics of employees in SHOPR may not be affected by their justice perceptions. However Courtesy was also correlated with interactional justice perceptions of employees, $r (200) = .242$, $p = .001$, the relationship was positive and weak in linearity. The civic virtue of employees was also found to be correlated with interactional justice perceptions as well, $r (200) = .241$, $p = .001$.

4.4 The Proportion of Variance Accounted for by Predictor Variables on OCB

After all correlational tests were done to proceed with regression analysis, the next stage was to determine whether there were interactional effects among the predictor variables and overall OCB as well as its dimensions. But before going into the actual computation of values all the necessary pre-conditions of regression tests were checked accordingly.

Table-15- Multiple regression analysis of Overall OCB and Predictor variables

Model	Unstandardized Coefficients		Standardized Coefficients		
	B	Std. Error	Beta	t	Sig.
(Constant)	51.569	6.033		8.547	.000
Organizational identification	.322	.196	.116	1.642	.102
Job involvement	.637	.156	.294	4.082	.000
Distributive justice	-.237	.150	-.116	-1.585	.115
Procedural justice	.147	.139	.089	1.059	.291
Interactional justice	.311	.117	.205	2.663	.008

a. Dependent Variable: Overall OCB

As the above table showed, there were two significant predictors independent, namely job involvement and interactional justice to overall OCB. It was an important finding that the predictor variables had been considered as an indicator of overall OCB, according to the ANOVA table results revealed, $F(5,196)=11.43$, $p<.001$, $R^2 =.226$, which showed that the overall regression model was a good indicator of independent variables   which significantly predicts the dependent variables. Well, after the multiple regression analysis were calculated, Job involvement has been found statistically significant predictor of overall OCB,$\beta = .637, t(202) = 4.022, p < .001$, which indicated that   the increase in participants job involvement tends to increase overall OCB levels with a significant change in at least by 4.022 points per one unit change in the independent variable. And interactional justice was also found statistically significant predictor of overall OCB, $\beta = .311$, $t(202) = 2.663, p < .001$. This is also an indication that the increase in participants' interactional justice perceptions could bear   actual change of the overall OCB level at least by .311 if all other variables remained constant. From this instance, it is possible to conclude that the predictor variables (Organizational identification, Job involvement, Distributive justice, Procedural justice and Interactional justice) combined influence was significantly explained 22.6% of the variance contributed to the overall OCB level. The rest 77.4% of variance to predict overall OCB level was attributed to extraneous variables outside of the current study variables, however, it is also important to consider that 3.4% of variance was formerly found by socio-demographic variables as to predict overall OCB level. Including this, the general predicting power of the variance explained by all independent variables reached in to 26%.

Table- 16-Stepwise Regression results of the predictor variables with model summary

Model	R	R Square	Adjusted R	Std. Error of the Estimate
1	.392[a]	.153	.149	11.00749
2	.448[b]	.201	.193	10.78844

a. Predictors: (Constant), Job involvement

b. Predictors: (Constant), Job involvement, Interactional justice

Because there were two significant predictor variables to overall OCB, stepwise regression analysis was computed as to show the strong predictors with their interaction and table-22-clearly indicated that job involvement has been significantly predicted, $F(202)=36.032$, $p<.001$, $R^2 =.153$. Which was shown that 15.3% of the total variance explained by independent variables was contributed from Job involvement solely. The rest 20.1% of the variance was the combined effect of Job involvement and Interactional justice altogether $F(202) = 25.766$, $p<.001$, $R^2=.201$. Generally, overall OCB has been predicted from organizational identification, job involvement, distributive justice, procedural justice and interactional justice perceptions.

Table -17- Canonical Correlation results for Predictor variable sets& OCB dimensions

Dimension Reduction Analysis

	Correlation	Eigenvalue	Wilks Statistic	F	Num D.F	Denom D.F.	Sig.
1	.534	.400	.663	2.761	30.000	766.000	.000
2	.236	.059	.928	.724	20.000	637.742	.803
3	.092	.009	.983	.277	12.000	510.922	.993
4	.082	.007	.991	.280	6.000	388.000	.946
5	.044	.002	.998	.	.	.	.

Set 1&2 Standardized Canonical Correlation Coefficients(with functions)

Variable	1	2	3	4	5		1	2	3	4	5
OI	-.349	-.571	.438	-.782	.083	A	-.455	-.362	-.667	-.392	.948
JI	-.528	.805	.378	.297	-.391	C	-.438	-.086	.668	-.526	-1.002
DJ	.148	-.390	-.453	-.166	- .978	S	.011	-.763	-.453	.073	-.540
PJ	-.179	-.608	.190	1.082	.415	Co	-.068	.739	-.826	.183	-.612
IJ	-.404	.400	-.838	-.514	.457	Civ	-.247	-.31	.566	1.023	.431

Set 1 &2 Canonical Loadings(with functions)

Variable	1	2	3	4	5		1	2	3	4	5
OI	-.681	-.464	.365	-.433	-.013	A	-.877	-.086	-.284	-.213	.313
JI	-.795	.355	.226	.180	-.397	C	-.880	.024	.276	-.226	-.313
DJ	-.333	-.381	-.468	.089	-.719	S	.218	-.783	-.389	.192	-.388
PJ	-.649	-.485	-.199	.543	.096	Co	-.600	.483	-.449	.364	-.269
IJ	-.681	.013	-.693	-.070	.225	Civ	-.696	-.052	.141	.701	.035

Set 1&2 Cross Loadings(with functions)

Variable	1	2	3	4	5		1	2	3	4	5
OI	-.363	-.102	.030	-.031	.000	A	-.467	-.019	-.023	-.015	.004
JI	-.423	.078	.019	.013	-.004	C	-.468	.005	.023	-.016	-.004
DJ	-.177	-.084	-.039	.006	-.008	S	.116	-.173	-.032	.014	-.004
PJ	-.345	-.107	-.016	.038	.001	Co	-.319	.107	-.037	.026	-.003
IJ	-.363	.003	-.057	-.005	.003	Civ	-.371	-.011	.012	.050	.000

Proportion of variance explained by predictor variables and vice versa				
Canonical Variable	Set 1 by Self	Set 1 by Set 2	Set 2 by Self	Set 2 by Set 1
1	.419	119	.487	.138
2	.145	.007	.172	.008
3	.185	.001	.106	.001
4	.105	.001	.151	.001
5	.147	.000	.084	.000

As table -17- shown there canonical test was conducted to observe the relationship of predictor variables with dimensions of OCB. As the test indicated in categorized patterns and the first pair of canonical variate (function 1 to 5) has been accounted for, .534 with a statistically significant contribution, $F(30,766)=2.761, p<.001$. This result clearly points that organizational identification, Job involvement, Distributive justice, Procedural justice and Interactional justice perceptions of employees of SHOPR are all significantly predicated OCB dimensions. However, all the rest residual reduction of the analysis showed that, there were no significant relations ships between variates of the functions next to the first one, (function 2 to 5; function 3 to 5; and functions 4 to 5).That is a sign of all the variables that are reduced from the full set of predictor and outcome variables, i.e., excluding the five full set 1 and set 2 variable interactions were not considered significant to predict OCB dimensions and vice versa. The results of covariates were scored a canonical correlations of .236, .092 .082, .044 as in their order of computation. Because of that, the first canonical vicariates were taken to show the relationship of the pairs in advance. Given that, it is possible to conclude that all the five predictor variable sets in combination were significantly contributed to predict dimensions of OCB with different levels.

.   Based on standard canonical correlation coefficients of the independent and dependent variables, Organizational identification (-.394), job involvement (-.528) and Interactional justice (-.408) were perceived as indicators from their own sets of predictor variables. And this could be interpreted as the three variables were the better indicators of the within the boundaries of all predictor variables of the current study. On the other hand, from the outcome variables, Altruism (.455), Conscientiousness (.438), it is implicated that these two variables has been combined influences on OCB dimensions in accordance with the current study participants.

Regarding the canonical loading analysis, the correlation results that were above 0.30 were taken as an important signifiers to the the relationships between the two variable sets. Moreover, the canonical loading analysis was also shown that Job involvement (.795) was the strongest predictor from predictors set, Organizational identification (.681) and Interactional justice (.681) were the next strong predictors from predictors set as well as Procedural justice (.649) was the third highest contributor of predictor variables and finally Distributive justice perception (.333) was the last contributor of predictor variable sets. From the OCB dimensions, conscientiousness (-.880) has been the strong predictor from OCB variable sets, Altruism (-.877) was also the best predictor from all OCB dimensions from this variable set, Civic -virtue (-.696) was another important dimension to predict overall OCB from Its respective variable sets, Courtesy (-.600) was contributed to predict OCB. Sportsmanship dimension was not included from the strong predictors of overall OCB in this case.

To largely observe of the canonical variates of the independent variables in accordance with the outcome ones cross - loadings were measured. Based on that, Job involvement (-.423), organizational identification (-.363), Procedural justice (-.363) & Interactional justice (-.345) were correlated with OCB dimensions in different levels. However Procedural justice is not considered to be a robust predictor in this regard. In relation to Set two there are also strong indicators of among the dimensions to effectively shown correlational tendencies with the predictors. For instance, conscientiousness (-.468), Altruism (-.467), Civic virtue (-.371) &Courtesy (-.319) have shown a correlational relationship with predictor variables.

Furthermore, reduction analysis were also been examined in order to see the total variance explained by each variable sets and in combination. These results indicated that, 41.9% of the variance in predictor variables was contributed from the first canonical variate that it means organizational identification is a relatively good predictor from its own sets. In this regard, from the dependent variables, the first variate from the second set constituted about 48.7% of the variance explained by this set, that literary means altruism was a relatively good predictor with in the outcome variable set. Moreover, the actual shared variance that was explained between predictor variables and OCB dimensions is about 28.6% of variance accounted from the the first canonical variates, based on the square root of the canonical correlation between the predictors and OCB dimension sets . This indicated that ,the relationships between the current study's predictor variables and OCB dimensions is very important factors that must be taking as relevant to each other.

Concerning the redundancy index analysis, the proportion of variance in the predictors set explained 11.9% of the variates to be predict by OCB dimensions. In the same pattern, the OCB dimensions variable set has been explained 13.8% by the independent variable sets overall. This is an indication that the current study the predictor variables, Organizational identification, Job involvement, Organizational justice Perceptions of employees in SHOPR have been contributed at least 13.8 % of involving in showing extra role behavioral dimensions.

Chapter Five

Discussion

5.1 Introduction

Predictors of Organizational citizenship behavior (OCB) were the whole concern of the present paper. Towards different directions the research questions were addressed to observe the real experience of OCB induced situations or variable characteristics were assessed in depth. In different respects, the results of the research have assured that the level and interaction of organizational behavior related variables was indeed observed in the context of Secretariat of Ethiopia's Federal House of Peoples Representative (SHOPR) employees with different forms and strength. This experience to also true for different cross-cultural situations, both internationally and continentally. The reviewed literatures with both theoretical and empirical relevance proved that the current research variables, namely: OID, JI, OJ (DJ, PJ, IJ) and OCB and its dimensions are concretely interrelated in one or the other ways with of course the relationships were both mediated and may even independently associated by socio- demographic variables and number of other extraneous situations. Ultimately, it is very important to evaluate how employees' performances could be, overwhelmingly improved and contribute to achieve the fullest characterization of having Organizational citizenship behavior and its interplay with other important organizational behavior related factors. In general, the aim of this section is make a thoughtful discussion over the issues that were found with concrete evidences in the current research, and their significance as to communicate with the scientific world and referring other investigations in the area as to balance the realities of the study variables under different circumstances.

5.2 Socio-Demographic Variables and OCB

Socio -demographic characteristics have long been considered as one of the antecedents of OCB. In different literatures, there were proven which revealed that Socio - demographic variables had contributed to the presence of OCB. For instance, there are different research supports that were attributed to the role of socio demographic characteristics (race age, sex dissimilarities) on OCB (Qureshi, 2015).In this regard, the current research has not yet found such conclusions. By that, the major socio demographic variables were not significant in determining OCB. This was true for respondents Gender, Age, Educational background and Income. However SHOPR employees work experience found to be significantly related to overall OCB. This could be taken as some of the research indicated, it was possible to have some of an interlinked relationship between helpful behaviors as OCB and Employees length of service and educational level. (Pavalache-Ilie,2014). Generally, SHOPR employeys socio-demographic characteristics have not been found a significant indicator of Overall OCB except some instances like work experience. All the same, it is important to take no generaliazability of influences over the association between the two variables. But for the sake of the current research it was possible to conclude that Socio-demographic characteristics of employees did not predict the presence of overall OCB. This finding was in contrary to Yohannes's (2016) investigation, who contrasts different dimensions like work experience, level of education, teacher characteristics (personal goals, commitment, responsibility and economy), the nature of the teaching profession, empathy for students and communities and love for one's country and found them as basic reasons to display OCB behaviors in Bahir Dar town. In this regard, employees' socio demographic characteristics were not basically behind the extra role behavioral patterns in that there are other possible factors to lead them showing such behavioral patterns.

Next to that, the dimensions of OCB were also examined in order to clearly show that association between Socio-demographic characteristics and OCB. From this context, employees' Age group had significantly differed with Altruism dimension of OCB. It was also proved that employees Educational background has been associated with conscientiousness, which is a very important finding that of all the possible dimensions, educational experiences were possibly qualified to predict employees' overall perceptions of careful and systematic concerns to which it represents the awareness and performances of which in organizational contexts that are beyond the least possible necessities. It is better to consider that conscientiousness is developed through educational qualifications of SHOPR employees. This is an indication of how the SHOPR employees are taking care of their extra role behaviors in terms of the ideal responsibilities in the organization. This in turn could lead to the assumption that socio - demographic variables are relatively insufficient to predict OCB with the exception of some of the factors.

In sum, Socio-demographic variables are not found as a strong predictor of OCB in the context of SHOPR. However, some of the variables were associated with overall OCB and its dimensions. For that employee Work experience was found to be a significant indicator of overall OCB. Employees were in difference by their Age groups and Educational qualifications, to show altruism and the conscientiousness dimension of OCB respectively. All the supposition is discussed in terms of observing the actual influences of socio demographic variables generally as it was as important as it gets. From this instance, it was an important signal that the differences in participants socio-demographic charcteristics has not been affected the overall OCB levels. I am personally fascinating by this fact that different studies come up with different results to attribute such characteristics relevance for predicting helping behaviors in public organizations.

5.3 Organizational Identification and OCB

The relationships between organizational identification and OCB are found to be significant according to the findings of the current research. As it was also proven by different previous researches in the area that supports an employees' sense of oneness to their respective organizations has a tremendous impact on the way they are acting in different extra role behaviors like OCB in general.(Kane &Perrewé, 2012; Choi, Moon & Kim , 2014).The correlational results clearly showed that SHOPR employees OID was indeed one of the factors that were recognized as a contributing.It was also true that the relationships of Organizational identification and OCB are very critical to not only public organizations but also private ones with their contribution to the effectiveness of the organization through a strong commitment to helping behavior.(Srivastava & Madan , 2016).In this regard , the context of showed that they have relatively high Organizational identification capabilities that was significantly related with OCB, which it was very important to both the employees and the organization in general.

On the other hand, SHOPR employees Organizational identification perceptions were also siginificantly associated with OCB dimensions. It is related to the actual effect that were found by different research, as Dick,Wagner,Stellmacher & Christ (2004) asserted organizational identification has different aspects that serve interlinked with work related attitudes and behaviors. As the present research shown that Altruism, Conscientiousness,

Sportsmanship, Courtesy, Civic -virtue were significantly related to OID. Which it resembled that, employess OID is also a multple agent to affect the role and activities of different dimensions of OCB.In this regard it was not true for Sportsmansip dimenison of OCB ,which it takes individuals to show citizen-like posture in relationships with others by tolerating the inconveniences that are foreseeable and the capability of peoples to accept burdens of work without complaints and whims.(Organ, 1988).There was no significant relationship observed between SHOPR employees OID and their Sportsmanship level. No matter what employees' organizational identification may contribute to helping behaviors, it was not the case for Sportsmanship behavior. Overall, it is very important to notice that Organizational identification is considered by its positive contribution to Organizational citizenship behavior.(Demir, 2015).

Moreover, Socio demographic characteristics of SHOPR employees (i.e, Age, work experience, Educational status, Income) did not siginifcantly affect the relationships between Organizational identification and Overall OCB levels. This variable is best known for its moderation (mediating) effect in other organizational related variables.(Guangling, 2011).Its relationship with OCB eventually affected by other moderators like SHOPR background characteristics at large. From that it is possible to deduce that SHOPR employees had a good level of Organizational identification that was associated with their overall OCB level. This is an understanding that leads to the conclusion that, SHOPR employees Organizational identification was definitely associated with OCB, but not in the linearity of the strength of the relationship in general.

5.4 Job Involvement and OCB

Employees's job involvement is critical for organizational success that it is imperative to lead to organizational success and enhanced productivity in the organization. (Abdallah, Obeidat, Aqqad, Al Janini & Dahiyat, 2017). Assuming that, Job involvement is one of the worthwhile predictor of OCB,with direct or indirect relationship between the sub-scales of OCB and Job involvement .(e.g Diefendorff, Brown,Kamin,& Lord, 2002; Shragay &Tziner, 2011).Regrading that, SHOPR employees were also shown a siginificant relationship between Job involvement (JI) and Overall OCB. In this regard, Behtooee (2016) found that, the pridiction cababiliy of Job involvement is positive and significant among its effects on OCB.The correlation results of the current study has also been showed that OCB dimensions (Altruism,Conscientiousness,Sportsmanship,Courtesy, Civic – virtue) and Job invlovement has been siginificantly correlated.These relationships were not all positive.For instance, Sportmanship dimension of OCB has been negatively correlated with OCB.This is an indication that, even if it was weak in direction but the greater the job involvement could asscociated with the decrease in their capability to some how patiently stands with different tasks that needs no inconvenences.This may be relatevly seen with different research, as some cultural studies indicated that is there is a constructive outcome by the affective and behavioral involvement of employeees on some OCB dimensions and cognitive involvement inversely influence helping behaviors as well as these effects were somewhat experienced by employees's job category and gender.(Yutaka, 2012).

5.5Perceived Organizational Justice Dimensions and OCB

Organizational justice has long been considered as predictors of OCB.(e.g Jafari & Bidarian, 2012, Moorman, 1991).The fact that justice perceptions may have diffenet implications in helping behviors of the organizations was the cause to test it in the context of the current study site.To see the big picture in this regard it is important to caterorically observe the dimensions of Organizational justice inrelation to employees OCB level as to discussed it well.

5.5.1 Distributive Justice and OCB

Distributive justice has positioned to be a most important aspect of its predictabilty ability for cognitive, affective, and behavioral responses to particular significances.(Cohen-Charash & Spector, 2001).In this regrad, the role of distributive justice was found to be nonsignificant predictor of overall OCB.This may happen in two ways. First,the participants overall OCB level was relatively high, but this was not at least significantly predicted from employees perception of fair allocation of resources.Second, distributive justice perception may not directly related to predict OCB in the current research participants.And other researchers have proved that distributive and interactional justice are significantly associated with OCB.(Awang & Ahmad, 2015).This is one of the contexts that may create variations among different results in different contexts. That is why the current research is needed in general. From OCB dimensions, (Altruism, Conscientiousness,

Sportsmanship, Courtesy, Civic-virtue) distributive justice was significantly associated with Altruism and Conscientiousness levels. These relationships were exhibited at least different in employees perception of the process of fairness in resource allocation .Which create some predictive propensity in SHOPR employees helpful behaviors to their organization in terms constructively contributes to help other persons in day to day work problem (Altruism) and wise usage of organization's resources, time and etc.(Conscientiousness).This is a great indicator of Distributive justice in terms of the perceived fairness of outcomes that is related to its strong importance to organizational contexts.(Cohen - Charash & Spector, 2001).Including OCB dimensions, that are related to the outcome of the organization in general.

In conclusion, Distributive justice has not been significantly predicted overall OCB level of SHOPR employees with the dimensions, Alturism and Conscientiousness. However, it is wise to consider that the influence of Distributive justice on SHOPR employees in minimal.

5.5.2 Procedural Justice and OCB

Much research has been revealed that the dimensions of organizational justice, including procedural justice perception have diverse levels of effect on organizational outcomes, including OCB (e.g Jawahar & Stone , 2016). Considering that, SHOPR employees Procedural justice perceptions were significantly correlated.This result could be seen in alignment with other research evidences that justice perceptions in general are antecedents of OCB(Farh , 1997). Studies have also shown the influence of organizational justice in a straight and shared process specifically the procedural justice type and its effect on the source of individual dissimilarities that took around OCB role definitions.(e.g Kamdar, McAllister, & Turban, 2006).On the other hand, OCB dimensions(Altruism ,Courtesy, Conscientiousness, Civic-virtue) were also correlated with Procedural justice perceptions of employees. However, Sportsmanship dimension was not significantly associated with Procedural justice Perceptions of SHOPR employees. This is not noble for the case of the study, that the variable has not been determined to other OCB related factors in the present research.

5.5.3 Interactional Justice and OCB

Interactional justice has been conceptualized in relationship with the actual concern of the organization to include employee participation or say in the decision making process in general. The fact that this justice perception is very much important to uplift the performance of employees and the management at large.Regarding this, SHPOR employees interactionatial justice association between overall OCB was siginificant.Which it was positive and significant in terms of the quality of relationship. In this case, it is good to know that SHOPR workers are needed to be included in the decision making process of the organization in fair and just manner and this association are certainly contributing for the extra role behavior acted by employees.It is also true for other contexts in research,for instance in recent decades as a meta-anlaytic study shown that , interactional and procedural justice perceptions were considerd as strong pridictors of OCB.(Fassina, Jones & Uggerslev, 2008).Some evidences have also shown that ,there are significant relationships between distributive and interactional justice to OCB.(Awang & Ahmad , 2015).Additionally, other studies revealed that manager dependability could provide for the variation in the explanation of OCB other and above than interactional fairness.(Chaiburu & Lim ,2007).

On the other hand, dimenisons of OCB are examined in relation to interactional justice perceptions of SHOPR employees,and it stongly predicted them.However, Sportmanship dimension was not sufficently predicted from interactional justice perceptions. This dimesion was also been failed to predict other justice related dimensions in the case of the current study. In this regard it is best to acknowledge that, the major characteristic of interactional justice is that it is unaffected by the individual self-interest.(Ladebo ,2014). Generally, Bies (2015) indicated that, interactional justice is a very influential idea that provide very good insight to describe organizational justice dynamics all the way through the whole organizational processes and outcomes. These were also expressed in SHOPR employees and the results were indicated that, Interactional justice perception is one of the predictors of OCB in this public organization.This is simply means that there was a strong association between the two variables, as some studies have brought that dimensions of organizational justice perceptions have diverse magnitude but influence to organizational consequences including OCB.(Jawahar & Stone , 2016)

5.6 Overall Influence of the Predictor Variables on Employees OCB

As it was delivered with many evidences, there are many predictors OCB that proves to be as an antecedent and factors that are having a systematic relationship with this variable. This includes personality related factors, Attitude related factors (justice perceptions, role perceptions, motivation etc, leadership styles work group, and the like could be mentioned. Regarding the current study, the influence of each predictor variable was examined to see the effect they are brought to the determine SHOPR employees OCB level. Based on that, there was a significant model summary that indicated the overall predictive variable power to significantly predict SHOPR employees OCB and its dimensions. By that, at least 22.6 % of the total variance of SHOPR employees OCB levels were due to the influence of the predictor variables. This is true to many evidences which stipulate that diverse job attitudes are strong predictors of its presence. (Organ& Ryan (1995).From that general depiction of the model summary,each varible were observed to see the combined effect they are caused. In this regard, Job involvement has been found statistically significant predictor of overall OCB, and interactional justice was also found statistically significant predictor of overall OCB of SHOPR employees. This is to show that all other predictor variables (Organizational identity, Distributive justice and Procedural justice) were having little influence in a combined level to generally determine the SHOPR employees general OCB. As far as the prediction power concerned, SHOPR employees' job involvement level separately was contributed for 15.3% of variance to explain over all OCB levels. On the other hand, 20.6% of variance of SHOPR employees overall OCB level was explained by the combined effects of Job involvement and Interactional justice altogether. This result may be seen in alignment with antecedents OCB and its dimensions, which have a basis with behavioral and attitudinal predispositions. (LePine, Jeffrey,Ertiz,Amir,Johnson & Danie, 2002). The overall influence in terms of OCB dimensions has also been observed by detailed analysis.

By and large, overall OCB consequences (efficiency, productivity, customer satisfaction, reduced costs, and unit level turn over) as Podsakoff, Whiting, Podsakokoff & Blume, (2009), could be determined through most of the current study variables. As most of employees' related performances' are manifestations of human beings at work together, which can be understood in association using basic human nature, attitudes and psychological needs. (Micheal, 2001). This was also true for the actual results gained from the current research as SHOPR employees Socio-demographic characteristics (Gender, Age, Work experience, Educational background and Income),Organizational identification (OID), Job involvement(JI),Distributive justice(DJ),Procedural justice(PJ),Interactional justice(IJ) were investigated to actually determine their effect. As most of them significantly related to Overall OCB and its dimensions. This could be seen in relation to theoretical and empirical evidences that are hypothesized attitudinal and behavioral and cognitive factors that are considered as predispositions of helpful and extra-role behaviors in an organization.(e.g, Gilovich, Keltner, Chen & Nisbet, 2016; Pierce & Maurer, 2009;Masterson, Lewis ,Goldman &Taylor , 2000 ; Areyee , Budhar &Chen , 2002; Tajfel and Turner , 1986; Moorman, 1991).

Furthermore, the predictor variables of this research were proved that overall OCB levels of SHOPR employees are powerfully influenced by different variables that are based upon the organizational conditions. This is also true for different cross- cultural research, especially in public organizations. (Pavalache - Ilie, 2014).

Chapter Six

Conclusion, Implications and Recommendations

6.1 Conclusion

After having a critical investigation of SHOPR employees' in relation to the study variables the following Important findings were found.

1.   Most of the Socio-demographic variables are not associated with overall OCB. For instance. Employees were not significantly varied by their Gender, Age groups, Work experience, Educational status and Monthly income. However, SHOPR employees work experience was found to be significantly related to Overall OCB. Regarding the dimensions of OCB, employees were significantly varied by their Age groups and Educational status in terms of Altruism & Conscientiousness.

2.   Organizational identification has a statistically significant relationship with SHOPR employees Overall OCB. Other than that, most of the dimensions of OCB were also significantly associated with Organizational identification except Sportsmanship, which was not statistically associated with employees OID.

3.   Job involvement was not significantly associated with SHOPR employees Overall OCB. There were also a significant relationship between OCB dimensions and Job involvement with an exception of the pattern of this relationship with Sportsmanship dimension which is an inverse type of relationship.

4. Concerning employees Organizational justice perceptions, generally two of the three dimensions were significantly associated with overall OCB. More specifically,

4.1   Distributive justice perceptions of SHOPR employees were not significantly correlated with their overall OCB. About OCB dimensions, only Altruism & Conscientiousness were significantly associated with Distributive justice perceptions.

4.2   Procedural justice has significantly associated with overall OCB. On the other hand, from the dimensions of OCB, Altruism, Conscientiousness, Courtesy, Civic- virtue were significantly correlated with SHOPR employees Procedural justice perceptions. However, sportsmanship dimension was not significantly correlated with Procedural justice perceptions of employees.

4.3   Interactional justice perceptions of SHOPR employees did have significant relationships with overall OCB level. The four dimensions OCB, Altruism Conscientiousness, Courtesy, and Civic -virtue were significantly related to SHOPR employees Interactional justice perceptions.

5.   The proportion of variance explained by independent variables to overall OCB were found to be fit in prediction model summary as 23.2% of the total variance was explained from these variables. The actual prediction power of the study variables, however, was varied accordingly, that is, Job involvement was predicted 15.3% of the total variance and the combination of job involvement and Interactional justice perceptions of the employees explained 20.6% of the total variance accounted by independent variables to significantly predicted overall OCB level. Furthermore, the dimensions of OCB were also predicted from the canonical variates of predictor variables. In this case, the relationship was proved by canonical correlation results of, .534 and with a shared proportion of variance accounted for was reached in to 28.6% multidimensional. This is clearly an indication of the strong contribution of Organizational identification, Job involvement perceived Organizational justice perceptions to determine OCB dimensions presence. From all these variables, Job involvement, organizational Identification, Interactional justice and procedural justice perceptions of employees are relatively good predictors of OCB dimensions. The reduction index analysis showed that the magnitude of relationships in the two sets of variables predicted by a redundancy of 11.9% of the variates to be predict by OCB dimensions that are to explain independent variable sets and, a redundancy of 13.8 was the total proportion of variance that was explained by predictor variables sets in order to predict OCB dimension sets. From these findings , The relationship of two variable sets was indeed important and has been considered as a pertinent one.

6.2 Implications

The results of the current study have tremendous implication on different aspects that are contributing to the scientific understanding of organizational behavior related constructs. In addition to that, the practical nature of the research results has also been influenced the applicability of variables in organizational contexts as a whole. The significance of the study is based upon the theoretical and practical implications it has instigated as part of the findings. That is the common characteristics of this part of the paper. Furthermore the idea of this study   results will be synthesized concept by concept to deal with the systematized relevance of the products of research findings.

6.2.1 Theoretical Implication

The consequence of this research is critical in showing the theoretical advantage that it has brought in the local (Ethiopian) context and as part of the universal nature of the researched variables. In light of that, Organizational behavior related constructs have long been digested with areas of behavioral and social sciences in detail globally. However, in a cross cultural context like Ethiopia, there are few research in dealing with such factors with rigorous and multidimensional approaches. Here is the relevance of the current study comes.

That is the uses of the study could be seen in three ways in alignment with theoretical implications: Primarily, the ideal propositions of the study variables are indeed workable to the nature and reality of the Ethiopian public service contexts. The characterization of OCB as a construct and theoretical perspective proved to be predicted from other attitudinal and behavioral related perceptions of employees as Organizational identification, Job involvement, and organizational justice. The theoretical foundations of OCB are also evidenced to enhance an organizational pattern in relations to employees' active duties and extra role behaviors. The nature and antecedents of OCB have also been inconclusive with the contexts of the research areas specifically and as a way of the expressions of it in the Ethiopian context in general. This is an indication of how the basic characteristics of the construct are carefully developed and serves as a platform to examine cross cultural contexts.

On the second point, the Ethiopian context has a researchable public service to examine organizational behavior related variables with deep and scientific analysis. In this regard, the real observation in the current study has brought a good implication to widely test theoretical formulations of organizational based attitudinal, behavioral and cognitive patterns of OCB and predictor variables like it has used in the present study are often a good indicator of the interrelations of variables at theoretical level and with their influence in further development. This has created a breakthrough environment for better understanding of the local context that shapes the human behaviors in relation to cross culturally diverse situation. It is also an advantage of the theoretical advancements of OCB related variables at indigenous level solutions and knowledge transfer.

Finally, the nature of the current study variables is very complex and multifaceted to fully comprehend and analyses with the conceptual scopes. The relevance of the present study in this case is, it has shown the technical aspects of the nature of different theoretical explanations that are focused to synthesize the essence of the constructs. As the whole process of the current research was basically depending on the ideas of different scholars that were accountable for the development of the theories and different perspectives that shaped the nature of the study variables. This was heavenly delivered in the current study with empirical evidences and the nature of the study variables has also been shown that it has matched with organizational contexts of SHOPR as one of the country's public services. Furthermore, the idealistic presumptions of these variables were tested and it has shown that all the study variables theoretical natures must be improved in the future. With the dynamic worldview of individuals, the conceptualizations of the study variables were well defined with the nature of vibrant organizational contexts especially in the western contexts. In relation to that, the current study has determined to investigate the theoretical nature of the study variables and has found that theoretical explanations of such constructs needs to be further improved to include the wider world. From that case in point, cross culturally the justifications of this variable must be advanced with total considerations of the basic differences of individual and group behavioral dynamics. For this to happen, the research outcomes served as a means to the researchers, especially in the local context to start proving the applicability of theoretical foundations of the study variables and related organizational organizational behavior constructs.

6.2.2 Practical Implication

In the research tradition of social behavioral sciences, practical significance and consequences of the study are essential elements. Based on this, the current study has conveyed diverse implications. For instance, it clearly identified that employees of an organization may have an acceptable level of OCB without the expected performances of an organization. That is, the variation between organizational performance and individual interests are integrated to be expressed in terms of employees OCB levels. In this regard, it was found that, the employees OCB levels are high with the predictive power of some selected variables(Organizational identification, Job involvement, perceptions of Distributive justice, Procedural justice, Interactional justice).Practically, that are indicated very important connections of the organizational behavior dynamics to uplift and improve organizational achievements. However, this may not be the case with the organizational level performance, i.e. individual employees have contributed to their respective organization's performance in such a way that if the organization is ready to be helped or achieved in general. Otherwise, the context of the organization must not be forgotten before seeing the practical relevance of the interrelationships of the predictor variables and consequences of OCB as to show its clearer pictures.

In this respect, the findings of the study are generally of assistance to better understand the organization in terms of behavioral patterns of employees and to adjust ones work context with the recognitions of the values of attitudinal and behavioral variables to enhance extra role behaviors in the organization. This will also lead to consequences of the effective OCB level of employees, like, employee performance, less withdrawals and absenteeism, low employee turnover rates, and effective reward allocation decisions. Additionally the findings of the study have also shown that, the overall OCB level of employees if considered with the interrelationships of this variable with predictor variables as in the study, will enhance the organizational level of OCB consequences like customer satisfaction, productivity, efficiency and reduced costs.Yet, the broader research investigation with the considerations of other extraneous variables that are not explored in the current study must be measured with the contexts of the organization or other macro level analysis.

In the other hand, the organization in the study or other public organizations in the country are practically benefiting from the findings of the study starting from: the practical applications of enhancing employees' organizational identification levels by showing respect and rational action in each organization as way to their employees to develop sense of oneness to their respective organization. This could be done in two ways, first by creating the conducive atmospheres to the employees of the organization in different respects. Secondly, it is wise to use employees' intrinsic motivations as to naturally lead them to sense their organization as their best place to realize their potential and ability. This is a practical relevance that comes from having a sufficient OCB level of the employees in order to take care of their organization additional to the formal duties of their work.

Another practical implication of the current study is that it showed how much it is important to get employees better involved with their job by facilitating all the preconditions of practical job involvement induced situations or skills that are leading to effectively contribute for enhanced OCB levels. From the study findings, the better the employees are involved in to their jobs, the more they are equipped with extra role behaviors in their day to day life. This is one practical notion that, organizations have played a pivotal role to introduce different mechanisms that are in the scientific paths of human behavior in an organization. Furthermore, it is also important to take into account the findings of the study to better understand the levels of employees' extent to actually involve in their jobs. It has led to create better understanding of the OCB levels of employees as a means to positively influence organizational activities.

Moreover, the practical relevance of studying organizational justice related perceptions to understand the influence it has produced to OCB is also an important step. This helps to give emphasis to the actual effect of the ideas of justice in work areas. That is if employees are not sensing that they are treated fairly in their organization, it is impossible to think of any extra- role activities including, OCB. Practical applications of justice induced packages intentionally in an organization is an important stage of the organization and decision making bodies in it. Research in the area are also benefited by considering the patterns of good organization in terms of employees' behavioral activities and the contributions they made. By considering the actual influences of justice perceptions as it is evidenced from the current study in relation to OCB.

In general, the actual relevance of the current study, findings weighs more than seeing the relationships of two variables. It has been considered interactional effects of the independent variables of the study to overall OCB and its dimensions. This is practically important to effectively understand the complete pictures of organizational context and other important issues. In this regard, the role of employees' characteristics in terms of leading them towards the actual effectiveness of them in OCB. In other directions, the interactions between each dependent variable could be delivered in the actual organizational performances which are related to these variables. The traditional contexts of organizations are composed of different patterns that are related to employees behavioral functioning in order to uplift the level of performances of employees.

The significance prediction power of the interaction of independent variables is helpful for practical approaches of different employment related motivational and capacity building activities to make sure that they are trusted their organizations and be effective in their extra role performances within the organization. Apart from that, it's also important to facilitate different occupational opportunities & trainings that are relevant to each organization based on the actual needs of employees by approaching the relevance of attitudinal and behavioral factors that are affected employees overall OCB level.

In general, the current study is very important to practically contribute in different respects. For instance, The study has revealed that OCB as a variable could be predicted from different other organizational constructs that are practically important for employees to be well performed and vibrant in the work place. Above all, the ability of clearly showing what are the most integrated relationships with employees - organizational interactions and the behavioral and attitudinal dynamics that are shaping these relationships will be helpful for practitioners and managerial activities by displaying the fact that employees could be raised or diminish their extra role behavior by the association of different predictors and the real effect they brought to the organization.

6.2.3 Organizational Implication

Specifically, organizations are expected to deal with their employees in different ways that could increase the performances and expectations. The results of the current research had also been important to organizations in general with many dimensions. For instance, the actual organizations are expected to be highly relying on their employees. The behavior of the employees correspondingly affected the performance of the organization. That is why research findings are important as a whole to search for a meaning of the change and improvement in organizational effectiveness. For that, public organizations are doing their work by the effort of their employees, the relevance of the current study to organizations therefore is it could bring new insight to the local context in relation to employees' management. The role of individual employees to create a comparatively better working environment could be affected by different variables like, organizational identification, Job involvement and organizational justice perceptions. This is due to the level of expectations and trust in their organizations. The organization with a standard public service must fulfill its employee's sense of belongingness and fairness attitudes that are directly contributing to the whole performances and to OCB. By that, it is increasing the effectiveness and efficiency of organizations and better picture of the customers they are treated with. In other words, the current study findings and the aim of the research do have an outstanding contribution to an organizational level of analysis and practice to create active employees who are dependable in their organization with the positive attitudes towards the organizations they are working in.

In detailed description, organizational behavior related variables have been examined to get maximum outcome in relation to employee engagement in their organization. Organizations could be benefited by applying the accepted principles of handling of employees in their day to day functioning. If that occurs, the satisfaction of employees could be raised, the turnover rates could be minimized and the achievement of the organization could be elevated. This is also helpful to change the trends of public organizations traditional efficiency patterns by their employees. In this regard, everything must be supported by having concrete evidences of research like the present one.

In general, organizations are expected to acquaint themselves with performances of their employees, if they are ready to be familiar with the influences of attitudinal and behavioral factors that are contributing for the inception and the presence of OCB and other helping behaviors. The Ethiopian public organizational context also is beneficial from having such a research outputs that are focused by different psychological patterns that are relevant in working places. The customary outlook in organizational related interactions must have been changed with a lot more quality based assessments to which effectively produced employees with active participation. The behavioral arrangements of organizations are possibly shaped within relationships of subordinates and managerial positions, which are easily affected by variables that are dependent on having different characteristics within the dynamics.

6.2.4 Research & Policy Implication

Depending on the actual implication of the current study, research in the area could be benefited with both the direction and outcomes of organizational behavior researches especially in Ethiopian with individual and group level emphasis. It has also a tremendous influence on advanced levels of analysis in organizational settings to applied research and development. Predictors of OCB are not only specified by the current study variables, but also extensively be explored with different factors that are not covered. The research interests in this context may be inspired by the outcomes of the current study. Because the study has been observed the deep interconnections between actual works related expectations of employees in different level with their effect on Overall OCB levels and the dimensions. These findings are considered to be a baseline for comprehensive studies in the area with the actual benefits of organizational behavior explanations and effective utilization of human resources

The other relevance of the present study in relation to research is that it clearly showed how the selected variables could be examined by different statistical approaches and quantitative method in general. Based on the purpose of the study, different research may be conducted for organizational behavior related variables. However, as the present study totally focused on the quantitative analysis of predictor variables of OCB, the investigation is possible to contribute to different research, with a detailed understanding of the natures of the varies in terms of the patterns of the variables and the change they are encountered due to different manipulations in the process of understandings.

Additionally, the wide-ranging outputs of the current study are probably a breakthrough in the Ethiopian context except for some previous researches in the area. That was a great effort made to deliver the holistic identifications of knowledge products that are unique to the local environment. Especially, the idea of organizational behavior arrangements are not well researched, compared with other parts of the world. The current study's attempt is breaking this trend with the assistance of different but little previous studies. Other research could be advanced by the referencing the current study and its general determinations. Furthermore, academic research will also expect to be inspired by the standpoints of the current study in creating better understandings of the predictors of OCB with attitudinal, behavioral and cognitive factors in focus. It will also be a reliable source of the literature review with a strong empirical evidences in broad-spectrum.

In accordance with policy implication, the current study could give a great relevance to employment related policy recommendations in the public services of both the national and regional contexts. In place of the cross -cultural dynamics, organizational behavior related analysis must be incorporated with policy preparation, analysis and evaluation process. The importance of the current study in this regard is, it gives a clear picture as to what must be done to effectively mobilize employees of the public services in relation to both in role and the extra role behavioral patterns. This in turn gives a space for policy makers and even for organizational leaders as to integrate the demands of employees for any particular gain in the behavioral outlooks of the organization and the general structural issues that affects the effectiveness and efficiency of employees. It's also important to get a practical understanding of attitudinal, behavioral and cognitive aspects of employees before any policy governance was made.

The other most important feature in relation to policy is that, most of the efforts that are held to address employee issues are not well substantiated with research evidences. And that is produced at high vacuums to further considerate of the difficulties of employees in workplaces in general. This generates misunderstandings and low rates of performances among employees and their supervisors as a whole. But as the current study depicts, an organized condition is shaped the context of organizational behavior patterns of employees to show them the participatory level of performances in their day to day activities of work. It could be well addressed by the effective uses of employees related policy frames with a standard principle of employee behavioral change arrangements. Apart from that, any effort which is trying to seek ideal organizational effectiveness and efficiency should take a great deal of concern to employees extra role behaviors. As well it is important to think through different factors that are having psychological consequences. This must be the concern of policy level of analysis in the public domain that are backing the public interest and the general handlings of employees in organizational contexts. In sum, employees related policies of governments or other stakeholders have to critically watch over the organizational behavior variables and their prominence in creating active and responsive employees of the public services. It could be done by considering the role of Organizational identification, Job involvement, Distributive justice, Procedural justice and Interactional justice perceptions of employees in relation to Organizational citizenship behavior forms and its application to the public service.

6. 2. 5 Limitation of the Study

This research relied upon the correlational research design assumptions that are not strict in controlling and manipulations of variables to get the desired results. The process of the study has been put with the acceptable approaches of probability sampling rationales. In between there are different shortcomings observed studies like this in general. The first one is that it has no strict sense of seeing the causal relationships of variables in the process of the research, for instance the relationships of variables in the study does not necessarily implied to causation. However, the research output has clearly shown the magnitude of the relationships as well as variabilities of predictors and the outcome variable. On the other side, the current research solely depends on quantitative research methods that is focused on the expression of variables in terms of their parametric tendency rather than in-depth analysis of study variables in terms of different dimensions, it has also not tried to triangulate different methodological approaches to validate the research outputs.

In relation to the computation and description of the variables, the major concern of the current study is to actually see the interactions of different variables and their effect on the outcome variable especially organizational related variables only in one public service organization. That does not enable the research to make comparisons among other public/organizations in accordance with the study variables implications towards different situations.

As a final point, the current study has a tremendous impact considering organizational behavior related factors in Ethiopian public service organizations. Especially , from the stand point of the major realities of employees' conceptions and behavioral patterns regarding work and extra role activities. For this part, the major challenge is to exactly attribute the responses from participants as an end by itself. Because self- reporting questionnaires are administered with the postulation of passive–stimulant research participants, there may be flaws and deceptions in the real life situation. That also rests as the limitation of this research. With all the contemplations of such factors, the current research has its own strengthens and inadequacies that are part and parcel of scientific research principally with the operational aspects of the investigation. The determinants of the quality of the quantitative correlational scheme was not yet been compromised by the present research and throughout its process in general however. Other than that, constraints in time, finance and other important resources made the research to be conducted in limited context. The shortcomings in these respects were influenced the scope of the current research number of organizations to be included in the study.

6.3 Recommendations

6.3.1 Recommendations for Future Research

Because all the efforts of the current study are not enough to conclude about the broad features of predictors of OCB, in the future different research are needed with a variety of perspectives and approaches of investigation. In this regard the following recommendations are made:

First, The predictors of OCB must be expanded other than the current research conceptual scopes. That is, different variables like, motivation, Personality, Leadership styles Attitudes, Role perceptions, Work groups, Task characteristic and etc. This will help to fully understand the psychological dynamics of organizational behavior and employees' characterization.

Second, the approach which was applied in the current study was a quantitative method. In the future, such organizational behavior related variables must be rigorously studied by using qualitative or mixed approaches. As all the research approaches have their own pros and cons, using an eclectic approach to investigate organizational related variables could give a wide range of understanding in the area. This is also important to get an in-depth analysis of the research variables and to triangulate the findings with different approaches. Other than that, the ideas and impressions of employees could be part of the detailed analysis of different research approaches with unconditional considerations of the responses of the study participants.

Third, the concepts of in role and extra role behaviors must be discovered in detail. In organizations, employees are basically doing their formal work obligations and extra role activities. These role patterns need to be critically investigated with research outcomes that are to be seen the categorizations of the activities with the relationships and the effect that are brought by these activities.

Fourth, the comparative study of predictors of OCB in private and public sectors in Ethiopia is another area of research in the future. In this regard, the researchers could focus on different aspects of organizational pattern in the two sectors with employees' behavioral appearances to display and use extra role behaviors day to day and for the benefit of organizational success. Because changes in different organizations could lead to further understandings of each sector with the effects of these behavioral factors in dealing with best possible ways that are discussed in variety of contexts.

Fifth, even in the public services, the study of extra role behaviors must be studied with large scale samples with many organizations involvement. This is very important to see the variables in wider situation and the differences among employees with in greater participants. Moreover, it's also gives researchers to see the role of OCB in different contextual dimensions as to generalize with the Ethiopian organizational context.

Sixth, consequences of OCB are also be another research areas that could be done in the future. In this regard, the actual performances of employees in OCB must be investigated as part of the aspects that are recognized as the best possible effects of OCB in organizational contexts. This will add to the scientific considerations of the real life end product of OCB and other helping behaviors in organizations and elsewhere as well.

References

Abdallah A.B, Obeidat,B.Y., Aqqad N.O., Al Janini M.N.k ., and Dahiyat S.E. (2017). An Integrated Model of Job Involvement, Job Satisfaction and Organizational Commitment: A Structural Analysis in Jordan's Banking Sector. *Communications and Network, 9*, 28-53. doi:10.4236/cn.2017.91002

Akintayo, D. I. and Oyebamiji M.A. (2011). Some Psychological Factors as Predictors of Perceived Workers' Productivity in private Organizations in Nigeria. *World Journal of Education, 1*(2), 30-38. doi:10.5430/wje.v1n2p30

Albert S.,Ashforth E.,and Dutton E. (2000). Organizational Identity and Identification:Charting New Waters and Building New Bridges. *Mangement Review, 25*(1), 13-17.doi: 10. 5465/ amr. 2000.2791600

Ali Nadir. (2016). Effect of Organizational Justice on Organizational Citizenship Behavior: A Study of Health Sector of Pakistan. *Review of Public Administration and Management, 4*(3), 2-9. doi:10.4172/2315-7844.1000198

Alizadeh Z.,Darvishi S.,Nazari K., and Emami M. (2012). Antecedents and Consequences of Organisational Citizenship Behaviour (OCB):. *Interdisciplinary Journal of Contemporary Research in Business , 9*(6), 494-505.

Allameh M., Alinajimi S., and kazemi A. (2012). The Effect of Self-concept and Organizational Identity on Organizational Citizenship Behavior (A Case Study in Social Security Organization of Isfahan city). *International Journal of Human Resource Studies, 2*(1), 2162-3058. doi:10.5296/ijhrs.v2i1.1119

American Psychological Association. (2010). *Publication manual of the American Psychological Association* (6th ed.). Washington, DC: American Psychological Association.

Antil, H. (1984). Conceptualization and Operationalization of Involvement. *Advances in Consumer Research, 11*, 203-209.

Appelbaum M. et.al. (2018). Journal Article Reporting standards for Quantitative Research in Psychology:The APA Publication and Communaications Board Task Force Report. *Americal psychologist, 73*(1), 3-25. doi:10.1037/amp0000191

Ashforth BE., and Mael F. (1989). Social Identity Theory and the Organization. *Academy of Management Review, 14*(1), 20-39. Retrieved from http://www.jstor.org/stable/258189

Ashforth BE.,Harrison H., and Corely G. (2008). Identification in Organizations: An Examination of Four Fundamental Questions. *Journal of Management(Abstract), 34*(3), 325-374. doi:10.1177/0149206308316059

Awang R., and Ahmad W. R. (2015). The Impact of Organizational Justice on
    Organizational Citizenship Behavior in Malaysian Higher Education.
    Mediterranean Journal of Social Sciences , 6(52), 674-678.
    doi:10.5901/mjss.2015.v6n5s2p674

Bachrach,D.G.,Bendoly,E.,and Podsakoff,P.M. (2001). Attributions of the "Causes" of
    Gruop Performance as an alternative expalntion of relationships between
    organizational citizenship behavior and organizational performance. *Journal of
    Applied Psychology, 86*(6), 1285-1293. doi:10.1037/0021-9010.8.6.61285

Baldwin, S. (2006). *Organizational justice.* Brington, UK: Institute of Employement
    Studies.

Bartels, J. (2006). Organizational identification and
    Communication:Employees'Evaluations of Internal Communication and Its Effect
    on Identification at Different Organizatioanal Level. *Doctoral dissertation.*
    University of Twente.

Bayarcelik B.E and Findikli A.M. (2016). The Mediating Effect of Job Satisfaction On The
    Relation Between Organizational Justice Perception And Intention To Leave.
    Procedia - Social and Behavioral Sciences , 235, 403-411.
    doi:10.1016/j.sbspro.2016.11.050

Beheshtifar M., and Emambakhsh M.(2013). Relation between Job Involvement and
    Service Quality. *Applied mathematics in Engineering, Management and
    Technology, 1*(4), 35-39.

Behtooee, L. (2016). A model for explanation of social capital in organizations,
    psychological empowerment,A model for explanation of social capital in
    organizations, psychological empowerment,job involvement, and organizational
    citizenship behavior. *International Journal of Advanced and Applied Sciences, 3*(5),
    80-87.

Bertolino, M. (2006). The Contributions of Organizational Justice Theory to Combating
    Discrimination. *Discrimination : perspectives de la psychologie.*
    doi:http://urmis.revues.org/223

Bez, O. (2010). Organizational Citizenship Behavior and its Relationship with Major
    Attitudinal Factors: A Comparative Study between Two Police Regions of Turkish
    National Policeof Turkish National Police of Turkish National Police. *PhD
    Dissertation.* Rechmond, Virginia, USA.

Bies, J.R. (2015). Interactional Justice: Looking Backward, Looking Forward. In C. S. S.
    Russell. (Ed.), *The Oxford Handbook of Justice in the Workplace.*
    doi:10.1093/oxfordhb/9780199981410.013.4

Brown, P. (1996). A meta-analysis and review of organizational research on job involvement. *Psychological Bulletin, 120*(2), 325-255. doi:10.1037/0033-2909.120.2.235

Bukhari, U. (2008). Key Antecedents of Organizational Citizenship (OCB) in the Banking Sector of Pakistan. *International Journal of Business and Management, 3*(2), 106-115.

Cappelli P., and Rogovsky N. (1998). Employee Involvement and Organizational Citizenship: Implications for Labor Law Reform and "Lean Production#x201D;. *ILR Review, 51*(4), 633-653. doi:10.1177/001979399805100405

Chahal H.,and Mehta S.(2010). Antecedents and Consequences of Organizational Citizenship Behavior(OCB): A Conceptual Framework in Reference toHealth CareSector. *Journal of Services Research, 10*(2), 26-43.

Chaiburu D.S and Lim S.A. (2007). Manager Trustworthiness or Interactional Justice? Predicting Organizational Citizenship Behaviors. *Journal of Business Ethics , 83*, 453-467.

Chattopadhyay, P. (1999). Beyond Direct and Symetrical Effects:The Influence of Demographic Dissimilarity on Organizational citizenship behavior. *Acadamy of Management journal, 42*(3), 273-287.

Chen CC and Chiu SF. (2009). The mediating role of job involvement in the relationship between job characteristics and organizational citizenship behavior. *J Soc Psychol, 149*(4), 474-494. doi: 10.3200/SOCP.149.4.474-494

Chiaburu,D.S.,Oh,I-S.,Berry, C.M.,Li,N.,and Gardner,R.G. (2011). The five factor model of personality tarits and organizational citizenship behaviors:A meta-analysis. *Journal of Applied Psychology, 96*(6), 1140-1166. doi:10.1037/a0024004

Chiu Su-F.,and Tsai C.M. (2006). Relationships Among Burnout, Job Involvement, and Organizational Citizenship Behavior. *The Journal of Psychology, 140*(6), 517-530. doi:10.3200/JRLP.140.6.517-530

Choi K., Moon K., and Kim K. (2014). A cross-sectional study of the relationships between organizational justices and OCB: Roles of organizational identification and psychological contracts. *Leadership & Organization Development Journal, 35*(6), 530-554. doi:10.1108/LODJ-08-2012-0103

Choi, N. (2009). Collective Dynamics of citizenship behavior:What Group Charcreristics Promote Group-level helping? *Journal of Management Studies, 46*(8), 1396-1420. doi:10.111/j.1467-6486.2009.00851.x

Chughtai, A. A. (2008). Impact of Job Involvement on In-Role Job Performance and Organizational Citizenship Behaviour. *Institute of Behavioral and Applied Management*, 169-183.

Cohen-Charash Y., and Spector E. P. (2001). The Role of Justice in Organizations:A Meta-Analysis. *Organizational Behavior and Human Decision Processes, 86*(2), 278–321. doi:10.1006/obhd.2001.2958

Colquitt A.J. (2012). Organizational Justice. In W. kozoloski (Ed.), *The Oxford Handbook of Organizational Psychology* (Vol. 1, pp.26-547). New York: Oxford University Press.

Colquitt A.J.,Colon E.D.,Wesson J.M.,Porter O.L.H Christopher and Ng Y.K. (2001). Justice at the Millenum : A meta analytic Review of 25 Years of Organizational Justice Research. *Journal of Applied Psychology, 86*(3), 425-445. doi:10.1037//0021-9010.86.3.425

Colquitt A.J.,Greenberg J.,and Zapata-Phelan P.C. (2005). What is Organizational Justice? A Historical Overview. In a. C. Greenberg G. (Ed.), *Handbook of Organizational Justice* (pp. 3-59). Lawrence Erlbaum Associations, Inc.

Constitution of the Federal Democratic Republic of Ethiopia. (1995). Addis Ababa: Birhan and Selam Printing Press.

Cropanzano R., Bowen D.E and Gilliland S.W. (2007). The Management of Organizational Justice. *Academy of Management Perspectives*, 34-48.

Demir, k. (2015). The Effect of Organizational Justice and Perceived Organizational Support on Organizational Citizenship Behaviors: The Mediating Role of Organizational Identification. *Eurasian Journal of Educational Research*(60), 131-148. doi:10.14689/ejer.2015.60.8

Dick R., Wagner U., Stellmacher J., and Christ O. (2004). The utility of a broader conceptualization of organizational identification: Which aspects? *Journal of Occupational and Organizational Psychology, 77*, 171–191. Retrieved from www.bps.org.uk

Diefendorff M.J., Brown J.D.,Kamin M.A.,and Lord G.R.. (2001). Examining the roles of job involvement and work centrality in predicting organizational citizenship behaviors and job performance. *Journal of Organizational Behavior(Abstract), 23*(1), 93-108. doi:10.1002/job.123

Diefendorff M.J.,Brown J.D.,Kamin M.n.,and Lord R.G. (2002). Examining the Role of Job involvement and Work Centrality in Pridicting Organizational citezenship behaviors and Work performance. *Journal of Organizational Behavior, 23*, 93-108. doi:10.1002/job.123

Dong C. S.,& Sue F. (2015). Government Employees's Organizational Citezenship Behavior:The impact ofPublic Motivation,Organizational Identification and Subjective OCB Norms. *International public management Journal, 20*(4), 531-559. doi:10.1080?10967494.2015.1037943

Donovan J. (2001). Work motivation. In O. S. Anderson N. (Ed.), *Handbook of Industrial Work & Organizational Psychology:Organizational Psyachology* (Vol. 2, pp. 53-77). London: SAGE Publications.

Dwirosanti N. (2017). Impact of Transformational Leadership ,Personality and Job involvement to Organizational Citezenship Behavior. *International Journal of Human CapitalManagement, 1*(2), 27-36.

Eatough,E.M.,Chang,C-H., Miloslavic,S.A.,and Johnson,R.E. (2011). The relationships of role Stressors with organizational citizenship behavior:A meta-analysis. *Journal of Applied Psychology, 96*(3), 619-632. doi:10.1037/a0021887

Edwards R. and Peccei R. (2007). Organizational identification: Development and testing of a conceptually grounded measure. *European Journal of Work and Organizational Psychology , 16*(1). doi:Organizational identification: Development and testing of a conceptually grounded measure

Ehrhart G.M. (2004). Leadership and Procedural Justice Climate as Antecedents of Unit-Level Organizational Citizenship Behavior. *Personnel Psychology, 57*(1), 61-94. doi:10.1111/j.1744-6570.2004.tb02484.x

Ehrhart,M.G.,and Naumann,S.E. (2004). Organizational citizenship behavior in work Groups: Agropu norm Approach. *Journal of Applied Psychology, 89*(6), 960-974. doi:10.1037/0021-9010.8.9.6.960

Eib, C. (2015). Processes of Organizational Justice:Insights into the perception and enactment of justice. Malmö, Sweden: Holmbergs.

Ekmekçi, A. (2011). A study on involvement and commitment of employees in Turkey. *Journal of Public Administration and Policy Research, 3*(3), 68-73.

Elovainio M.,Kivimäk M., and Vahtera J. (2002). Organizational Justice: Evidence of a New Psychosocial Predictor of Health. *American Journal of Public Health, 92*(1), 105-108.

Erturk A.,Yilmaz C., and Ceylan A. (2004). Promoting orgniaztional citizenship behaviors:Relative effects of job satisfaction. *METU studies in Development*, 189-210.

Eyerusalem, A. (2016). Employee Equity Perception Towards Performances Management and its Association With Organizational Commitment with References to Employess of Federal Government Ministeries of Ethiopia. *Master's thesis*. Addis Ababa University. Retrieved from www.aau.edu.et(Institutional Repository)

Farh J., Earley and Lin S.C. (1997). Impetus for Action: A Cultural Analysis of Justice and Organizational Citizenship Behavior in Chinese Society. *Administrative Science Quarterly), 42*(3), 421-444. doi:10.2307/2393733

Fassina E.N.,Jones D.A and Uggerslev L.K. (2008). Meta-analytic tests of relationships between organizational justice and citizenship behavior: testing agent-system and shared-variance models. *Journal of Orgaizational Behavior*, 805-828. doi:10.1002/job.494

Federal Negarit Gazette of The Federal Democratic Republic of Ethiopia. (2015). *Secretariat of the House of Peoples' Representatives Re-establishment Proclamation*. Addis Ababa.

Fields, D. L. (2002). *Taking the measure of work: A guide to validated scales for organizational research and diagnosis*. Thousand Oaks: Sage Publications.

Flávia de S.,Fábio, de A., and Ana L . (2017). Organizational identification among Brazilian public employees: a study of the cultural sector. *Review of Business Management, 19*(64), pp. 289-306. doi:DOI: 10.7819/rbgn.v19i64.2899

Folger R., and Cropanzano R.(1998). *Organizational Justice and Human Resource Management*. London: Sage pubilications,Inc.

Francis, U. (2014). Organizatinal Citezenship Behavior and Demographic Factors among Oil Workers in Nigeria. *IOSR Journal OF Humanities And Social Science(IOSR-JHSS), 19*(8), 87-95.

Gelfand J.M.,Erez M.,and Aycan Z. (2007). Cross-Cultural Organizational Behavior. *Annu. Rev. Psychol, 58*, 479-514.

Getahun A., and Lehal R. (2015). Organizational Citizenship Behavior In Relation To Social Capital in North West Region of Ethiopian Electric Power. *International Journal of Applied Research, 1*(11), 1044-1051.

Gilkar A., and Darzi A.(2013). Job Involvement - Sense of Participation - Job Satisfaction: A Triangular Framework. *IOSR Journal of Business and Management , 6*(6), 41-47. Retrieved from iosrjournals.org

Gilovich T., Keltner D., Chen S.and Nisbet R.E. (2016). *Social Psychology* (4 ed.). New York: W. W. Norton & Company, Inc.

Gioia A., Shultz M., and Corely G. (2000). Organizational Identity, Image, and Adaptive Instability. *ACAD MANAGE REV, 25*(1), 63-81. doi: 10.5465/AMR.2000.2791603

Govender S., and Parumasur SB. (2010). The Relationship between Employees motivation and Job involvement. *AJEMS NS*(3).

Griffin, E. (2011). A first look at Communication Theory. In *Social Exchange Theory of John Thibaut & Harold Kelley* (8 ed., pp. 196-205). McGraw-Hill.

Guangling, W.(2011). The Study on Relationship between Employees' Sense of Organizational Justice and Organizational Citizenship Behavior in Private Enterprises . *Energy Procedia, 5,* 2030-2034. doi:10.1016/j.egypro.2011.03.350

Guangling, W. (2011). The Study on Relationship between Employees' Sense of Organizational Justice and Organizational Citizenship. *Energy Procedia, 5,* 2030–2034. doi:doi:10.1016/j.egypro.2011.03.350

Hakim W.,Nimran U.,Haerani S.,and Alam S. (2014). The Antecedents of Organizational Citizenship Behavior (OCB) and TheirEffect on Performance:Study on Public University in Makassar, South Sulawesi, Indonesia. *IOSR Journal of Business and Management, 16*(2), 05-13.

Haridakis., Robyn E., and Paul. (2008). Development of an Organizational Identification Scale:Integrating Cognitive and Communicative Conceptualizations. *Journal of Communication Studies, 1*(3/4), 105-126.

Harper J.P. (2015). Exploring forms of organizational citizenship behaviors (OCB):antecedents and outcomes. *Journal of Management and Marketing Research, 18,* 1-16.

Hassan, A. (2002). Organizational Justice AS a Determinant of Organizational Commitment. *Asian Academy of Management Journal, 7*(2), 55-66.

Hassan, S. (2012). Employee Attachment to Workplace: A review of Organizational and Occupational Identification and Commitment. *International Journal of Organization Theory and Behavior, 15*(3), 383-422.

Hatch J., and Schultz M. (1997). Relations between organizational culture,identity and image. *European Journal of Marketing,* 356-365.

He H., Zhu W., and Zheng X. (2014). Procedural Justice and Employee Engagement: Roles of Organizational Identification and Moral Identity Centrality. *Journal of Business Ethics, 122*(4), 681-685.

Hegtvedt, K. A. (2006). Justice Framework. In P. j. Burke(Ed), *Contemporary Social Psychological Theories* (pp. 46-70). Stanford, California: Stanford University Press.

Ho C.,Oldenburg B., Day G., and Sun J. (2012). Work Values, Job Involvement, and Organizational Commitment in Taiwanese Nurses. *International Journal of Psychology and Behavioral Sciences, 2*(3), 64-70. doi:10.5923/j.ijpbs.20120203.02

Hogg, M. A. (1999). Group Decision Making. In Manstead, & Hewstone (Eds.), *The Blackwell Encyclopedia of Social Psychology A-Z* (3 ed., p. 267). Blackwell Publishers Inc.

Hui, C., Lam, S.S.K., & Law, K.S. (2000). Instrumental values of organizational citizenship behavior for promotion: A field quasiexperiment. *Journal of Applied Psychology, 85*, 822-828.

Humphreys M., and Brown D. (2002). Narratives of Organizational Identity and Identiification:A case Study of Hegemony and Resistance. *Organizational Studies, 23*(3), 421-447.

Ickes, W. (1999). Organizations. In Manstead, & Hewstone (Eds.), *The Blackwell Encyclopedia of Social Psychology* (3 ed., p. 425). Blackwell Publishers Ltd.

Ilies, e. (2009). Personality and citizenship behavior: The mediating rele of job satisfaction. *Journal of Applied Psychology, 94*(4), 945-959.

Ilies, R., Nahrgang,J.D and Morgeson,F.P. (2007). Leader-member Exchange and citizenship and Citizenship behaviors:A meta-analysis. *Journal of Applied Psychology, 92*(1), 269-277. doi:10.1037/0021-9010.9.2.1.269

Iqbal K. H., and Tasawar A. (2012). Impact of Organizational Justice on Organizational Citizenship Behavior: An Empirical Evidence from Pakistan. *World Applied Sciences Journal, 19*(9), 1348- 1354. doi: 10.5829/idosi.wasj.2012.19.09.750

Iqbal Z.M.,Rehan M., Fatima M. and Nawab S.(2017). The Impact of Organizational Justice on Employee Performance in Public Sector Organization of Pakistan. *International Journal of Economics & Management Sciences*, 431. doi:10.4172/2162-6359.1000431

Jafari P., and Bidarian S. (2012). The relationship between Organizational justice and Organizational citizenship behavior. *Procedia - Social and Behavioral Sciences, 47*, pp. 1815-1820.

Jahangir N.,Akbar M.M.,and Haq M. (2004). Organizational Citezenship Behavior:Its Nature and Antecedents. *BRAC University Journal, I*(2), 75-85.

Jawahar M.I and Stone H.T. (2016). Do career satisfaction and support mediate the effects of justice on organizational citizenship behaviour and counterproductive work behaviour? *Canadian Journal of Administrative Sciences(Abstract), 34*(4), 189-194.

Jex M.S., and Britt W.T. (2008). *Productive Behavior in Organizations* (2nd ed.). New Jerssey: John Wiley & Sons, Inc.

Jhonson D., Morgeson P., and Hekman R. (2012). Cognitive and affective identification: Exploringthe links between different forms of socialidentification and personality with work attitudes and behavior. *Journal of Organizational Behavior, 33*, 1142 – 1167 . doi:10.1002/job.1787

Johnson D,. and Morgeson P. (2005). Cognitive and Affective Identification in Organizational Context. *64th Annual Meeting of the Academy of Management*, (pp. 1-6). Honolulu.

Jones C., and Volpe H. (2010). Organizational identification: Extending our understanding of social identities through social networks. *Journal of Organizational Behavior*, 1-22. doi:DOI: 10.1002/job.694

Jong and Gutteling . (2006). Relations between organizational identity, identification and Organizational objectives:An empirical study in municipalities. *Afstudeerartikel voor de opleiding Toegepaste Communicatiewetenschap*, 1-20.

Judge A.T., and Colquitt A.J. (2004). Organizational Justice and Stress: The Mediating Role of. *Journal of Applied Psychology, 89*(4), 395-404. doi:10.1037/0021-9010.89.3.395

Kamdar,D., McAllister,D.J., andTurban,D.B. (2006). "All in a Day's Work":Hw follower individual Differences and Justice Perceptions Predict OCB Role definitions and Behaviors. *journal of Applied Psychology) , 94*(4), 841-855. doi:10.1037/0021-9010.9.1.4.841

Kane K., and Perrewé L. (2012). Differential effects of identification on extra-role behavior. *International Journal of Career Management, 25*(1), 25-42. doi:10.1108/13620431211201319

kanugo, N. (1982). Measurment of Job and Work involvement. *Journal of applied Psychology, 67*(3), 341-349.

Karaolidis, D. (2016). Organizational Citezenship Behavior in The Greek Public Sector. *Master's thesis*. University of Mecedonia.

Klotz AC., Bolino MC., Song H., and Stornell J. (2017). Examining the nature,causes,and consequences of profiles of organizational citizenship behavior. *Journal of organizational Behavior*, 1-19. doi:10.1002/job.2259

Knippenber D.S. (2006). Organizational identification versus organizational commitment:Self-definition, social exchange,and job attitudes. (27), 571-584. doi:DOI: 10.1002/job.359

Ladebo J.O, Awotunde M.J and AbdulSalaam-Saghir. (2014). Coworkers' and Supervisor Interactional Justice: Correlates of Extension Coworkers' and Supervisor Interactional Justice: Correlates of Extension Personnel's Job Satisfaction, Distress, and Aggressive Behavior. *39*(6), 691-719. doi:10.1177/1059601114551605

Lam W.L.,Liu Y.,&Loi R. (2016). Looking intra-organizationally for identity cues:Whether perceived organizational support shapes employees' organizational identification. *human relation, 69*(2), 345-367. doi:10.1177/0018726715584689

Lam,S.S.K.,Hui,C.,&Law,K.S. (1999). Organizational citizenship behavior:Comparing persepectives of supervisors and subordinates across for international samples . *Journal of Applied Psychology, 84*(4), 494-601. doi:10.1037/0021-9110.8.4.4.594

Le Pine A.,Jeffery A., Erez, Amir, and Jhonson,D. E. (2002). The Nature and Dimensionality of Organizational Citizenship Behavior:*Journal of Applied Psychology, 87*(1), 52-65. doi:10.1037//0021-9010.87.1.52

Lee K., and Allen J.N. (2002). Organizational Citizenship Behavior and Workplace Deviance:The Role of Affect and Cognitions. *Journal of Applied Psychology, 87*(1), 131-142. doi:10.1037//0021-9010.87.1.131

Lee, E.-S., Park, T.-Y., & Koo, B. (2015). Identifying organizational identification as a basis for attitudes and behaviors: A meta-analytic review. *Psychological Bulletin, 141*(5), 1049-1080. doi:10.1037/bul0000012

LePine,Jeffrey A.. Ertiz,Amir,Johnson., and Danie E. (2002). The nature and dimensionality of organizational citizenship behavior: A critical review and meta-analysis. *Journal of Applied Psychology, 87*(1), 52-65.

Li, N.,Liang,J.,and Crant, J.M. (2010). Therole of Proactive personality in job satisfaction and Organizational citizenship behavior:A relational persepective. *Journal of Applied Psychology(Abstract), 95*(2), 395-404. doi:10.1037/a0018079

Liliana D.G.,Claudio B., and Bernardo M.J. (2014). Spanish version of Colquitt's Organizational Justice Scale. *Psicothema, 26*(4), 538-544. doi: 10.7334/psicothema2014.110

Lin, Y. (2004). Organizational Identity and Its Implication on Organization Development. 809-8013.

Lind E.A, and Taylor R.T. (1988). Procedural justice in Organizations. In *The Social Psychology of Procedural Justice* (pp. 173-202). New York: Springer Science+Business Media .

Lind, A. (2001). Fairness Heruistic Theory: Justice Judgements as a Pivotal Cognitions in Organizational Relations. In Greenberg J. and Corpanazo R. (Ed.), *Advances in Organizational Justice* (pp. 56-89). Stanford Universty Press.

Lo. May-Chiun. (2009). Dimensionality of Organizational Citizenship Behavior (OCB)in a Multicultural Society: The Case of Malaysia. *International Business Research, 2*(1), 48-55.

Lonsdale, J. (2013). Interactional Justice and Emotional Abuse:Two Sides of the Same Coin? *Arts and Social Sciences Journal*, 1-6.

Ma E., Qu H., & Wilson M. (2013). The Affective and Dispositional Consequences of Organizational Citizenship Behavior. *Journal of Hospitality & Tourism Research, 40*(4), 399-431. doi:10.1177/1096348013503991

Mael, F., and Ashforth, B. E. (1992). Alumni and their alma mater: a partial test of the reformulated model of organizational identification. *Journal of Organizational Behavior, 13*, 103 – 123. doi:doi: 10.1002/job.4030130202

Malek, N. A. (2012). Relationship Between Demographic Variables and Educational Citezenship Behavior Among community College Lecuturers. In A. H. Ibrahim Duyar (Ed.), *Discretionary Behavior and Performance in Educational Organizations:The missing link in Educational Leadership and Management* (Vol. 13, pp. 117-138). Emrald Group Publishing Limited.

Mathur S. and Padmakumari. (2013). Organizational Justice and Organizational Citizenship Behavior among Store Executives. *Human Resource Management Research, 3*(4), 124-149. doi:10.5923/j.hrmr.20130304.02

Meal F.A., and Asforth B.E. (1995). Loyal from Day One:Biodata,Organizational identification, and Turnover among Newcomers. *Personnel Psychology, 48*(2), 309-332.

Micheal, W. A. (2001). The Human Team: Basic Motivations and Innovations. In A. Neil, O. S. Deniz, & S. K. Chockalingam (Eds.), *Handbook of Industrial, Work & Organizational Psychology* (Vol. 2, pp. 270-289). London: SAGE Publications.

Michele J..,Miriam E., and Zeynep A. (2007). Cross-Cultural Organizational Behavior. *Annu. Rev. Psychol, 58*, 479-514. doi:10.1146/annurev.psych.58.110405.085559

Mirzaee M., and Beygzadeh Y. (2017). Study of the Impact of Organizational citizenship behavior on Job involvement staff self desipline(Study case west Azerbajan Tax Office,Iran). *European Journal of Management and Marketing Studies, 2*(1), 11120. doi:10.5281/zenodo.806842

Missaye, M. (2016). Perceived Organizational Justice, Job Attitudes and Turnover Intention among Hospital Healthcare Workers in Gondar and Bahir-Dar. *Doctoral dissertation*. Addis Ababa University. Retrieved from www.aau.edu.et(Institutional Repository)

Moorman H. (1991). Relationship Between Organizational Justice and Organizational Citizenship Behaviors: Do Fairness Perceptions Influence Employee Citizenship? *Journal of Applied Psychology, 76*(6), 845-855.

Moorman, R. H., Blakely, G. L., & Niehoff, B. P. (1998). Does organizational support mediate the relationship between procedural justice and organizational citizenship behavior? A group value model explanation. *Academy of Management Journal, 41*, 351-357.

Murdvee M. (2014). *Social Exchange[powerpoint slides]*. Retrieved from Temarinet.com.

Nandan T., and Mohamed A.A. (2015). Organizational Justice and Organizational Citizenship Behavior: Mediating Role of Psychological Capital. *American International Journal of Social Science, 4*(6), 148-156.

Nelson, M.J., and Hrivnak, A.G. (2009). Organizational Citizenship Behavior and Performance:A Meta-Analysis of Group-Level Research. *Small Group Research, XX*(X), XX-XX. doi:10.1177/1046496409339630

Niehoff, B. P., and Moorman, R. H. (1993). Justice as a mediator between methods of monitoring and organizational citizenship behavior. . *Academy of Management Journal*, 527-556.

Nwibere, B. (2014). Interactive Relationship between Job Involvement, Job Satisfaction, Organisational Citizenship Behaviour, and Organizational Commitment in Nigerian Universities. *International Journal of Management and Sustainability, 3*(6), 321-340.

Organ D.W. (1997). Organizational Citizenship Behavior:It's Construct Clean-up Time. *Human Performance, 10*(2), 85-97.

Organ D.W, and Ryan K. (1995). A meta-analytic Review of Attitudinal and dispositional Predictors of Organizational citizenship behavior. *Personnel Psychology, 48*, 775-802.

Organ, D. (1988). *Organizational citizenship behavior: The good soldier syndrome.* Lexington, MA, England: Lexington Books/D. C. Heath and Com.

Organ, D. W., and Konovsky, M. (1989). Cognitive versus affective determinants of organizational citizenship behavior . *Journal of applied Psychology, 74*, 157-164.

Paddock.,Stephen W., and Layne. (2005). Organizational Justice Across Human Resource Management Descions. In G. P. Ford(Eds), *International Review of Industrial and Organizational Psychology* (Vol. 20, pp. 149-177). West Sussex,England: John Wiley & Sons Ltd.

Pavalache-Ilie, M. (2014). Organizational Citizenship Behaviour, Work Satisfaction and Employees' Personality. *Procedia - Social and Behavioral Sciences, 127*(22), 489-493. doi:10.1016/j.sbspro.2014.03.296

Pierce R. and Maurer J. (2009). Linking employee development activity, social exchange and organizational citzenship Behavior. *International Journal of Training and Development, 13*(3), 139-147.

Podaskof N.P., Podaskof, PM.,MacKenzie S.B., Maynes, T.D.and Spoelma ,T.M. (2014). Consequences of unit-level organizationalcitizenship behaviors: A review and recommendations for future research. *Journal of Organizational Behavior, 35*, S87–S119. doi:10.1002/job.1911

Podsakoff M.P., Ahearne M.,and MacKenzie B.S. (1997). Organizational Citizenship Behavior and the Quantity and Quality of Work Group Performance. *Journal of Applied Psychology, 82*(2), 262-270.

Podsakoff M.P., MacKenzie B.C.,Paine B.J and Bachrach G.D. (2000). Organizational Citizenship Behaviors: A Critical Review of the Theoretical and Empirical Literature and Suggestions for Future Research. *Journal of Management, 26*(3), 513-563.

Podsakoff NP,Whiting SW, Podsakokoff PM,and Blume BD. (2009). Individual - and organizational -level consequences of organizational citizenship behavior:a meta -analysis. *Journal of Applied Psychology(Abstract), 94*(1), 122-141. doi:10.1037/a0013079

Podsakoff, P. M., MacKenzie, S. B., Moorman, R., & Fetter, R. (1990). Transformational leader behaviors and their effects on trust,satisfaction, and organizational citizenship behaviors. *The Leadership Quarterly, 1*, 107-142.

Price, J. L., & Mueller, C. W. (1986). *Handbook of organizational measurement.* MA: Pittman: Marshfield.

Qureshi A.,Shahjehan A.,and Saifullah K. (2011). The effect of self-esteem and Organizational identification on organizational citizenship behavior:A case of Pakistani public sector university. *African journal of Business Management, 5*(9), 3448-3456.

Qureshi, H. (2015). A Study of Organizational Citizenship Behaviors (OCB) and its Antecedents in an Indian Police Agency. *Doctorial Dissertation.* Virginia Commonwealth University. Retrieved September 30, 2017, from https://www.researchgate.net/publication/296639798

Rabinowitz, S & Hall, D.T. (1977). Organizational research on Job involvement. *Psychological Bulletin, 84*(2), 265-288.

Ravasi D., and Rekom J. (2003). Key Issues in Organizational Identity andIdentification Theory. *Corporate Reputation Review* , 118-132.

Riketta, M. (2005). Organizational identifification: A meta-analysis. *Journal of Vocational Behavior, 66*(2), 358-384. doi:10.1016/j.jvb.2004.05.005

Rioux, S.M.,and Penner,L.A. (2001). The casuses of organizationalcitizenship behavior: A motivational Analysis . *Journal of Applied Psychology, 86*(6), 1301-1314. doi:10.1037.0021-9010.8.6.1306

Rizwan M., Khan D.J and Saboor F.(2011). Relationship of Job involvement with Employee Performance:. *European Journal of Business and Management, 3*(8), 77-85.

Rupp D., and Thornton M.(2017). *Oxford Biblographies.* doi:10.1093/OBO/9780199828340-0044

Rupp, E. (2001). Moral Virtues, Fairness Heuristics, Social Entities,and Other Denizens of Organizational Justice. *Journal of Vocational Behavio, 58,* 164-209. doi:10.1006/jvbe.2001.1791

Russell C., David E., and Stephen W. (2007). The Management of Organizational Justice. *Academy of Management Perspectives*, pp. 34-48.

Rustam P.,Farhad G., and Abdolmajid F. (2014). Explaining the Relationship Between Organizational Commmitment, Job Involvement and Organizatioanl Citizenship Behavior among Employees of Khuzestan Gas Company. *Indian Journal of Fundamental and Applied Life Sciences, 4*(S4), 150-158.

Saufi A.M., Kojuri A.M., Badi M., and Agheshlouei H. (2013). The Impacts of Organizational Justice and Psychological Empowerment on Organizational Citizenship Behavior: The Mediating Effect of Job Involvement. *International Journal of Research in Organizational Behavior and Human Resource Management, 1*(3), 116-135.

Saxena, S. and Saxena,S. (2015). Impact of Job Involvement and Organizational Commitment on Organizational Citizenship Behavior. *Int. J. Manag. Bus. Res., 5*(1), 19-30.

Saygin, H., and Muhammet. (2013). An Investigation of the Relationship between Social Loafing and Organizational Citizenship Behavior. *Procedia - Social and Behavioral Sciences* (pp. 206-215). Elsevier Ltd. doi:10.1016/j.sbspro.2013.10.487

Seo, Y. (2013). Job involvement of part-time faculty: exploring associations with distributive justice,underemployment, work status congruence, and empowerment. *PhD Dissertation.* Iowa. Retrieved from http://ir.uiowa.edu/etd

Seyyed M.,Mohammed D., and Kamil K. (2013). Studying the relationship between job involvement and organizational commitment with organizational citizenship behavior in management of the hajj pligramage in east Azerbaijan Province. *Technical Journal of Engineering and Applied Science, 3*(18), 2178-2183.

Shanker, M. (2004). Organizational Citizenship Behavior Dimensions in Indian Companies. *International Conference on Multidisciplinary Research & Practice, 1*(7), 24-28.

Sharma, A. (2016). Job Involvement: Attitudinal Outcome of Organizational Structural Factors. *European Journal of Training and Development Studies, 3*(4), 17-28.

Shragay D., and Tziner A. (2011). The Generational Effect on the Relationship between Job Involvement, Work Satisfaction, and Organizational Citizenship Behavior. *Revista de Psicología del Trabajo y de las Organizaciones, 27*(2), 143-157. doi:10.5093/tr2011v27n2a6

Skarlicki D.P.and Latham G.P. (1997). Leadership Training in Organizational Justice to Increase Citeznship Behavior Within a Labour Union: A Replication. *Personnel Psychology*, 617-633. doi:10.1111/j.1744-6570.1997.tb00707.x

Smith, C. A., Organ, D. W., and Near, J. P. (1983). Organizational citizenship behavior: Its nature and antecedents. *Journal of Applied Psychology, 68*(4), 653-663. doi:10.1037/0021-9010.68.4.653

Srivastava S. and Madan P. (2016). Understanding the Roles of Organizational Identification, Trust and Corporate Ethical Values in Employee Engagement–Organizational Citizenship Behaviour Relationship: A Study on Indian Managers. *Management and Labor studies*.

Srivastava, R. (2015). Multiple Dimensions of Organizational Justice and Work-Related Outcomes among Health-Care Professionals. *American Journal of Industrial and Business Management*, 666-685. doi:10.4236/ajibm.2015.511067

Staw M., and Kramer M.,. (2003). Research in Organizational Behavior: An Annual Series of Analytical Essays and Crtical Review. In a. K. Staw M., *Preface* (Vol. 25, pp. 1-52). Elsevier Ltd. doi:10.1016/S0191-3085(03)25001-2

Stets, J. E. (2006). Identity Theory. In P. j. Burke (Ed.), *Contemporary Social Psychological Theories* (pp. 88-111). Stanford University Press.

Steve M., and Thomas W. Britt. (2008). *Organizational psychology: a scientist-practitioner approach* (2nd ed.). Hoboken, New Jersey: John Wiley & Sons, Inc.

Suresh P., and Venkatammal P. (2010). Antecedents of Organizational Citizenship Behaviour. *Journal of the Indian Academy of Applied Psychology, 36*(2), 276-286.

Sweeney, P.D., & McFarlin, D.B. (1997). Process and outcome: Gender differences in the assessment of justice. *Journal of Organizational Behavior, 18*, 83-98.

Tajfel and Turner . (1986). The social psychology of Intergroup Behavior. In W. S. WG (Ed.), *Psychology of Intergroup Relations* (pp. 7-24). Chicago, IL, Nelson.

Tansky, W. (1993). Justice and organizational citizenship behavior: What is the relationship? *Employee Responsibilities and Rights Journal, 3*(3), 195-207. doi:10.1007/BF01419444

Temesgen, B. E. (2014). Anticedents and Consequences of Organizational Commiment Among Acadamic Staff in Public universities of Ethiopia. *Master's thesis*. Addis Ababa University. Retrieved from www.aau.edu.et(Institutional Repository)

Tepper,B.J.,Duffy,M.k.,Hoobler, J., and Ensley, M.D. (2004). Moderators of the
      Relationship between Coworkers'Organizational citizenship Behavior and Fellow
      Employees Attitudes. *Journal of applied Psychology, 89*(3), 455-465.
      doi:10.1037/0021-9010-8.9.3.455

Tepper,B.J.,Lockhart,D.,and Hobber,J. (2001). Justice ,citizenship,and role defintion
      effects. *Journal of Applied Psychology, 86*(4), 789-796. doi:10.1037/0021-
      9010.8.4.789

Tziner A., and Sharoni G. (2014). Organizational citizenship behavior, organizational
      justice, job stress, and workfamily conflict: Examination of their interrelationships
      with respondents from a non-Western culture. *Journal of Work and Organizational
      Psychology, 30*, 35-42. doi:DOI: http://dx.doi.org/10.5093/tr2014a5

Ufuk B., and Nejat B. (2015). Effects Effects of Organizational Identification on Job
      Satisfaction: Moderating Role of Organizational Politics. *Yönetim ve Ekonom,
      22*(2), 663-683.

Usmani, S., and Jamal S. (2013). Impact of Distributive Justice, Procedural Justice,
      Interactional Justice, Temporal Justice, Spatial Justice on Job Satisfaction of
      Banking Employees. *Rev. Integr. Bus. Econ. Res*, 351-383.

Verkuyten M., & Wolf D.A. (2002). Ethnic minority identity and group context:Self-
      descriptions, acculturation attitudes and group evaluations in an intra- and
      intergroup situation. *European Journal of Social Psychology, 32*, 781-800.
      doi:10.1002/ejsp.121

Vijayabanu C.,Govindarajan K., and Renganathan R. (2014). Organizational citizensjhip
      behavior and Job involvement of Indian Private sector Emploeeyes using VIsual
      Pls-Sem Model. *Management, 19*(2), 185-196.

Walumbwa,F.O.,Hartnell,C.A.,and Oke,A. (2010). Serevant leadership,Proedural justice
      climate, Service climate,employee attitudes,and organizational citizenship
      behavior:across-level investigation. *Journal of Applied Psychology, 95*(3), 517-529.
      doi:10.1037/a0018867

Whetten, A. (2006). Albert and Whetten Revisited: Strengthening the Concept of
      Organizational Identity. *Journal of Management Inquery Abstract), 15*(3).

Wicklund, R. A. (1999). Self-Categorization Theory. In Manstead, & Hewstone (Eds.).
      Blackwell Publishers Ltd.

Willi S., and Zainuba M. (2002). Justice and Organizational Citizenship Behavior
      Intentions:fair Rewards and Fair Treatment. *The Journal of Social Psychology, 14*,
      33-44. doi:10.1080/002245402096038

Woldemedhin, K. (2015). The Effectiveness of Job Rotation Practices in Improving
      Employess motivation,Commitment and Job Involvement: The case of Commercial

Bank of Ethiopia. *Master's thesis*. Addis Ababa University. Retrieved from www.aau.edu.et(Institutional Repository)

Wrk V.R., Bosohoff F.,and Cilliers F.(2003). The Pridiction of Job Involvement for Pharmacists and Accountants. *SA Journal of Industrial Psychology, 29*(3), 61-67.

Xenikou A. (2014). The Cognitive and Affective Componentsof Organisational Identification: The Roleof Perceived Support Values andCharismatic Leadership. *Applied Psychology: An International Review, 63*(4), 567-588. doi:10.1111/apps.12001

Xie, H. (2016). Review and Prospect on Interactional Justice. *Open Journal of Social Sciences, 4*, 55-61. doi:10.4236/jss.2016.41007

Yadav K.L and Yadav N. (2016). Organizational Justice: An Analysis of Approaches, Dimensions and Outcomes. *NMIMS Management Review, XXXI*, 14-40.

Yaffe,T.,and Kark,R. (2011). Leading by example:The case of leader OCB. *Journal of Applied Psychology, 96*(4), 806-826. doi:10.1037/a0022464

Yamane, T. (1967). *Statistics: An introductory analysis* (2nd ed.). New York: Harper & Row.

Yean F.T., and Yusof A.A.,. (2016). Organizational Justice:A conceptual Disscussion. *Procedia - Social and Behavioral Sciences, 219*, 798-803. doi: 10.1016/j.sbspro.2016.05.082

Yohannes, A. C. (2016). Organizational citizenship behavior (OCB) among teachers in Bahir Dar: Dimensions, antecedents, consequences and implications. *Doctoral dissertation*. Addis Ababa, Ethiopia. Retrieved from Retrived from www. aau.edu.et(Institutional Respository)

Yutaka, U. (2012). Effect of Job Involvement on Importance Evaluation of Organizational Citizenship Behavior. *International Journal of Business and Society, 13*(1).

Yutaka, U. (2015). *Recent Trends in Organizational Citizenship Behavior Research: 2010-2015*. Grant-in-Aid for Scientific Research. the Japan Society for the Promotion of Science (JSPS).

Zhang, D. (2011). Organisational Citizenship Behavior. *PSYCH761White Paper (OCB)*.

Zhangq Y.,Liao J., and Zhao J. (2011). Research on the Organizational Citizenship behavior Continuum and Its Consequences. *Front.Bus.Res.China, 5*(3), 364-379. doi:10.1007/s11782-011-0135-2

<u>APPENDICES</u>

Appendix-1 Questionnaires

Addis Ababa University
College of Education and Behavioral Studies
School of Psychology
Dear participants of the Study

Employees of the Public service are known to serve their Country and the people based on the expected responsibilities. However as a human being, there are different social and psychological interactions that are shaped the involvement and the perceptions of individuals towards their jobs. Although there are different explanations for that, most of them could be identified research. The major aim of this particular research therefore is, to investigate public service employees Organizations identification, Job involvement, Perceived organizational justice as predictors of Organizational citizenship behavior.

Regarding that, you are proudly selected as a study participant by assuming you pivotal role and with a full confidence of your active participation in the study. This research output is done in partial fulfilment of the requirements of the Postgraduate degree in Social psychology by a getting all the necessary information from the participants. And first and for most, I would like to give my gratitude for your patience and genuine participation.

Note

1. To give your responses please use "X" symbol.
2. Please try to respond to all the items.
3. If there is anything that is against your consent, you have full right to quit participating in the study.
4. About the confidentiality of participants' responses, the researcher shall take full responsibility with accountability.
5. You do not need to write your names in the questionnaire.

Thank You

Mutual consent form

I assure that, I am participating in this study with having the full information about the study and by my completest belief to give contribution aimed at the study.

Signature_____

Date_____

Part One- General Information

I. Gender   1. Male   ☐

                   2. Female   ☐

II. Age   1.18-29   ☐

(In Years)   2.30- 40   ☐

                   3.41- 50   ☐

                   4.51- 60   ☐

                   5. $\geq$ 61   ☐

III. Work Experience 1. 0-4   ☐

(In Years)   2.6-10   ☐

                   3.11- 15   ☐

                   4.16 - 20   ☐

                   5.21-25   ☐

                   6.26-30   ☐

                   7. $\geq$31   ☐

IV. Educational Background   1. Only Read & Write ☐

                           2.1-8   ☐

                           3.9-10   ☐

                           4.11-12   ☐

                           (Preparatory)

5. Technical & Vocational ☐   7. Undergraduate Degree ☐

               6. Diploma ☐   8. Postgraduate Degree ☐

V. Income   1. 500-1500 ☐   4.3501-4500 ☐   7. $\geq$6501 ☐

(In Birr)   2.1501-2500 ☐   5. 4501-5500 ☐

                   3.2501-3500 ☐   6.5501-6500 ☐

Part Two

No	Organizational Identification Scale	1 Strongly Disagree	2 Disagree	3 No Opinion	4 Agree	5 Strongly Disagree
1	When someone criticizes my organization, I feels like a personal insult.					
2	I am very interested in what others think about my organization.					
3	When I talk about my organization, I usually say we rather that they.					
4	This organizations success is my success.					
5	When someone praise this organization, it feels like a personal compliment.					
6	If a story in a media criticized my organization, I would feel embarrassed.					
	Job Involvement Scale	1	2	3	4	5
7	The most important things that happen to me involve my job.					
8	To me, my job is only a small part of who I am.(R)					
9	I am very much involved personally in my job.					
10	I live, eat and breathe my job.					
11	Most of my interests are centered around my job.					
12	I have very strong ties with my present job which would be very difficult to break.					

13	Usually I feel detached from my job.(R)						
14	Most of my personal life goals are job-oriented.						
15	I consider my job to be very central to my life.						
16	I like to be really involved in my job most of the time.						
Organizational justice Scale **Distributive justice**		1	2	3	4	5	
17	When considering the responsibilities that I have, I am fairly rewarded.						
18	When taking into account the amount of education and training that I have, I am fairly rewarded.						
19	When in view of the amount of experience that I have, I am fairly rewarded.						
20	When considering the amount of effort that I put forth, I am fairly rewarded.						
21	When considering the work that I have done well, I am fairly rewarded.						
22	When considering the stresses and strains of my job, I am fairly rewarded.						
Procedural justice		1	2	3	4	5	
23	I am not sure what determines how I can get a promotion in this organization.(R)						
24	I am told promptly when there's a change in policy, rules, or regulations that affects me.						
25	It's not really possible to change things around me.(R)						

26	There are adequate procedures to get my performance rating reconsidered if necessary.						
27	I understand the performance appraisal system being used in this organization.						
28	When changes are made in this organization, the employees usually lose out in the end. (R)						
29	Affirmative action policies have helped advance the employment opportunities in this organization.						
30	In general, disciplinary actions taken in this organization are fair and justified.						
31	I am not afraid to "blow the whistle" on things I find wrong with my organization.						
32	If I were subject to an involuntary personnel action, I believe my agency would adequately inform me of grievance and appeal rights.						
33	I am aware of the specific steps I must take to have a personnel action taken against mere considered.						
34	The procedures used to evaluate my performance have been fair and objective.						
35	In the past, I have been aware of what standards have been used to evaluate my performance.						

	Interactional justice	1	2	3	4	5	
36	When decisions are made about my job, the general manager treats me with kindness and consideration.						
37	When decisions are made about my job, the general manager treats me with respect and dignity.						
38	When decisions are made about my job, the general manager is sensitive to my personal needs.						
39	When decisions are made about my job, the general manager deals with me in a truthful manner.						
40	When decisions are made about my job, the general manager shows concern for my rights as an employee.						
41	Concerning decisions about my job, the general manager discusses the implications of the decisions with me.						
42	The general manager offers adequate justification for decisions made about my job.						
43	When making decisions about my job, the general manager offers an explanation that makes sense to me.						
44	My general manager explains very clearly any decisions made about my job.						

Organizational citizenship behavior Scale **Altruism**	1	2	3	4	5	
45	I help others who have been absent.					
46	I help others who have heavy workloads.					
47	I help orient new people even though it is not required.					
48	I willingly help others who have work-related problems.					
49	I am always ready to lend a helping hand to those around me.					
Conscientiousness	1	2	3	4	5	
50	Attendance at work is above the norm for me.					
51	I do not take extra breaks.					
52	I obey company rules and regulations even when no one is watching.					
53	I'm one of most conscientious employees.					
54	I believe in giving an honest day's work for an honest day's pay.					
Sportsmanship	1	2	3	4	5	
55	I consume a lot of time complaining about trivial matters. (R)					
56	I tend to make "mountains out of molehills". (R)					
57	I always focus on what's wrong rather than the positive side. (R)					
58	I always find fault with what the organization is doing. (R)					

59	I am the classic "squeaky wheel" that always needs greasing. (R)						
	Courtesy	1	2	3	4	5	
60	I take steps to try to prevent problems with other workers.						
61	I am mindful of how my behavior affects other people's job.						
62	I do not abuse the rights of others.						
63	I try to avoid creating problems for workers.						
64	I consider the impact of my actions on coworkers.						
	Civic virtue	1	2	3	4	5	
65	I attend meetings that are not mandatory, but are considered.						
66	I attend functions that are not required, but help the company image.						
67	I keep abreast of changes in the organization.						
68	I read and keep up with organizational announcements, memos, and so on.						

አዲስ አበባ ዩኒቨርስቲ

የትምህርትና ስነ-ባህሪይ ጥናት ኮሌጅ

የሳይኮሎጅ ትምህርት ክፍል

ውድ የዚህ ጥናት ተካፋዮች

የመንግስት ሰራተኞች በተለያዩ መስኮች ለአገራቸውና ለህዝባቸው በአገልግሎት ላይ የተመሰረተ ተግባር በማከናወን የሚጠበቅባቸዉን ሃላፊነት እንደሚወጡ ይታወቃል። ነገር ግን ሰዉ በተፈጥሮዉና በህይወት ልምድ በሚከሰቱ የተለያዩ የማህበራዊና ስነ-ልቦናዊ መስተጋብሮች አማካኝነት በስራ ላይ ያለዉ አመለካከትና ተሳትፎ እንደሁኔታዉ ሊለያዩ ይችላል። ለዚህ ደግሞ መሰረተ ብዙ ምክንያቶች ሊጠቀሱ ቢችሉም ዋና ዋናዎቹ ምን ምን እንደሆኑ በተለያዩ ጥናቶች ሊታወቁ ይችላል። የዚህ ጥናት ዋና አላማም በመንግስት መስሪያ ቤቶች ዉስጥ የሰራተኞችን ከተቋም ጋር የተያያዘ የስነ-ልቦና አንድነት፣የሰራ ተሳትፎ፣ የተቋማዊ ፍትህ ዕይታዎች ከመደበኛ ስራዎች ዉጭ የሆነ ተግባራትን በማሳደግ ረገድ የሚፈጥሩትን ተፅዕኖ አስመልክቶ ሰፋ ያለ ዳሰሳ ማከናወን ነዉ።

በመሆኑም እርስዎ የዚህ ጥናት ተሳታፊ ሆነዉ ሲመረጡ የሚያበረክቱትን ጉልህ አስተዋፅኦ ከግምት ዉስጥ በማስገባት ንቁና እዉነተኛ ተሳትፎ እንደሚያደርጉ በሙሉ ልብ በመተማመን ነዉ። ይህ ጥናትም በአዲስ አበባ ዩኒቨርስቲ የማህበራዊ-ሳይኮሎጅ ትምህርት የሁለተኛ ዲግሪ ማሟያ የሚያገለግል ግብዓት ለማግኘት የሚያስችለዉን መረጃ ከተሳታፊዎች በማግኘት አስፈላጊዉን ዉጤት ለማቅረብ ያስችላል። ስለዚህ በተዕግስት ለሚደርጉልኝ ትብብር ከወዲሁ ዎከፍ ያለ ምስጋናየን አቀርባለሁ።

ማሳሰቢያ

1. በጥያቄዎቹ ላይ መልስ ለመስጠት የ "X" ምልክት ያድርጉ።
2. በተቻለ መጠን ሁሉንም ጥያቄዎች ለመመለስ ጥረት ያድርጉ።
3. የርስዎን የግል ፍቃደኛነት የሚፈታተኑ ሁኔታዎች ካሉ በጥናቱ ላይ ያለመሳተፍ ሙሉ መብትዎ የተጠበቀ ይሆናል።
4. የዚህ ጥናት ተሳታፊዎች የሚሰጡትን ምላሽ ምስጢራዊነት አስመልክቶ አጥኝው ሙሉ ሃላፊነትን ከተጠያቂነት ጋር እንደሚወስድ ለማረጋገጥ እወዳለሁ።
5. በዚህ ጥናት ላይ ስም መጥቀስ አያስፈልግም።

አመሰግናለሁ።

የ*ጋራ ስምምነት ቅፅ*

እኔ በዚህ ጥናት የተሳተፍኩት ስለጥናቱ አስፈላጊዉን መረጃ በማግኘት እንዲሁም የበኩሌን ድርሻ ለማበርከት በማሰብ በራሴ ሙሉ ፈቃደኝነትና ይሁንታ መሆኑን አረጋግጣለሁ።

ፊርማ ---------------------

ቀን ---------------------

ክፍል-አንድ- አጠቃላይ መረጃዎች

I. ፆታ   1. ወንድ [ ]

           2. ሴት [ ]

II. ዕድሜ   1.18-29 [ ]

  (በዓመት)   2.30- 40 [ ]

           3.41- 50 [ ]

           4.51- 60 [ ]

           5. ≥ 61 [ ]

III.የስራ ልምድ   1. 0-4 [ ]

  (በዓመት)   2.6-10 [ ]

           3.11- 15 [ ]

           4.16–20 [ ]

           5.21-25 [ ]

           6.26-30 [ ]

           7. ≥31 [ ]

IV.የትምህርት ደረጃ   1.ማንበብና መፃፍ [ ]

             2.1-8 [ ]

             3.9-10 [ ]

             4.11-12(መሰናዶ) [ ]

             5.ቴክኒክና ሙያ [ ]   7. የመጀመሪያ ዲግሪ [ ]

             6.ዲፕሎማ [ ]   8. ሁለተኛ ዲግሪ [ ]

V.የገቢ መጠን   1. 500-1500 [ ]   4.3501-4500 [ ]   7. ≥6501 [ ]

  (በብር)   2.1501-2500 [ ]   5.4501-5500 [ ]

         3.2501-3500 [ ]   6.5501-6500 [ ]

ክፍል- ሁለት

ተ.ቁ	ከተቋም ጋር የተያያዘ የስነ-ልቦና አንድነነት	በጣም አልስማማም።	አልስማማም።	ምንም አይነት ሃሳብ የለኝም።	እስማማለሁ።	በጣም እስማማለሁ።
		1	2	3	4	5
1	ማንም ሰዉ የምሰራበትን ተቋም ሲኮንን እኔ በግል የተሰደብኩ ያህል ስሜት ይሰማኛል።					
2	ሌሎች ስለምሰራበት ተቋም ምን እንደሚያስቡ ለማወቅ ከፍ ያለ ፍላጎት አለኝ።					
3	ስለምሰራበት ተቋም ስናገር በአብዛኛዉ ጊዜ የእነሱ ከማለት ይልቅ እኔ ማለት ይቀናኛል።					
4	የምሰራበት ተቋም ስኬት የእኔም ስኬት ነዉ።					
5	የምሰራበትን ተቋም ሰዉ ሲያወድሰዉ የሚሰማኝ ስሜት እኔን በግል የማሞገስ ያህል ነዉ።					
6	የምሰራበትን ተቋም የሚኮንን ዘገባ በሚዲያ ብሰማ የሚረብሽ ስሜት የሚሰማኝ ይመስለኛል።					

	የስራ ተሳትፎ	1	2	3	4	5
7	በህይወቴ ዉስጥ የተከሰቱ በጣም አስፈላጊ ነገሮች ስራየን ያማክሉ ናቸዉ።					
8	ለእኔ የምሰራዉ ስራ ማለት የማንነቴ አነስተኛ ክፍል ብቻ ።					
9	በግሌ በስራየ ያለኝ ተሳትፎ በጣም ጥልቅ ነዉ።					
10	እኔ የምኖረዉ፣የምመገበዉና የምተነፍሰዉ ስራየን ነዉ።					
11	አብዛኛዎቹ የእኔ ፍላጎት የሚያተኩሩት በስራየ ላይ ነዉ።					
12	እኔ ከስራየ በጣም ጠንካራና ለመለያየት የሚያስቸግር ግንኙነት አለኝ።					
13	በአብዛኛዉ ጊዜ ከስራየ ጋር የመቆራረጥ ስሜት ይሰማኛል።					
14	ብዙ ጊዜ ከግል ህይወቴ ጋር የተያያዙ ግቦች ስራየን መሰረት ያደረጉ ናቸዉ።					
15	ስራየ ለእኔ ህይወት መሰረታዊ ጉዳይ እንደሆነ እመለከተዋለሁ።					
16	በአብዛኛዉ ጊዜ ከስራየ ጋር የጠበቀ ተሳትፎ እንዲኖረኝ እፈልጋለሁ።					
	የተቋማዊ ፍትህ ዕይታ	1	2	3	4	5
17	የተሰጡኝን ሃላፊነቶች አስመልክቶ ፍትሃዊ የሆነ ማበረታቻ አገኛለሁ።					
18	በትምህርትና ስልጠና ረገድ ያለኝን ልምድ ያገናዘበና ፍትሃዊ የሆነ ማበረታቻ አገኛለሁ።					
19	የስራ ልምዴን መሰረት ያደረገ ፍትሃዊ ማበረታቻ አገኛለሁ።					

20	በስራ ላይ የማዉለዉን ጥረት ባገናዘበ መልኩ ፍትሃዊ ማበረታቻ አገኛለሁ።					
21	በጥሩ ሁኔታ ስራዎችን የማከናዉን ከሆነ ፍትሃዊ ማበረታቻ አገኛለሁ።					
22	በስራ አጋጣሚ የማሳልፈዉን ዉጥረትና የስራ ጫና መሰረት ያደረገ ፍትሃዉ ማበረታቻ አገኛለሁ።					
23	በዚህ ተቋም ዉስጥ እድገት እንዴት ማግኘት እንዳለብኝ የሚወስነዉ ምን እንደሆነ እርግጠኛ አይደለሁም።					
24	የፖሊሲ፣የደንብና የመመሪያ ለዉጥ ሲኖር በአፋጣኝ እንዳዉቀዉ ይደረጋል።					
25	በእኔ ዙሪያ ያሉ ነገሮችን ለመቀየር የሚቻል አይደለም።					
26	አስፈላጊ ሆኖ ሲገኝ የስራ አፈፃፀም ዉጤት አሰጣጥን እንደገና ለማየት የሚያስችሉ በቂ የአሰራር ቅደም ተከተል አለ።					
27	በዚህ ተቋም ዉስጥ ያለዉን የዉጤት ግምገማ ስርዓት እረዳዋለሁ።					
28	በዚህ ተቋም ዉስጥ ለዉጦች ሲፈጠሩ በአብዛኛዉ በሰራተኞች ላይ ሸንፈት የሚያስከትሉ ናቸዉ ።					
29	የዚህ ተቋም የልዩ ተጠቃሚነት ፖሊሲዎች የሰራተኛ ዕድሎችን ለማሳደግ ረድተዋል።					
30	በዚህ ተቋም የሚወሰዱ የዲሲፕሊን እርምጃዎች በአጠቃላይ ፍትሃዊና ምክንያታዊ ናቸዉ።					
31	በምሰራብት ተቋም ዉስጥ ስህተት የሆኑ ነገሮችን					

	ሲያጋጥሙ· ከማጋለጥ ወደኋላ አልልም።				
32	ከራሴ ፍቃድ ዉጭ የሆነ ተግባር የሚያጋጥመኝ ከሆነ የምሰራበት ተቋም ስለቅሬታና ይግባኝ መብቶች በበቂ ሁኔታ እንደሚያሳዉቀኝ አምናለሁ።				
33	አላስፈላጊ የሆነ ተግባር ሲፈፀምብኝ መዉሰድ የሚኖርብኝን ዝርዝር ርምጃዎች አስመልክቶ እዉቀት አለኝ።				
34	የስራ አፈፃፀሜን ለመገምገም የሚከናወኑ ተግባራት ፍትሃዊና በመረጃ ላይ የተመሰረቱ ነበሩ።				
35	ከዚህ ቀደም በተከናወኑ የስራ አፈፃፀም ግምገማዎች ላይ ምን አይነት መለኪያዎች ጥቅም ላይ እንደዋሉ አዉቃለሁ።				
36	ስራየን የሚመለከቱ ዉሳኔዎች ሲተላለፉ የሚመለከተዉ የስራ ሃላፊ በትህትናና በጥንቃቄ ያስተናግደኛል።				
37	ስራየን የሚመለከቱ ዉሳኔዎች ሲተላለፉ የሚመለከተው የስራ ሃላፊ ክብሬን በጠበቀ መልኩ ያስተናግደኛል።				
38	ስራየን የሚመለከቱ ዉሳኔዎች ሲተላለፉ የሚመለከተዉ የስራ ሃላፊ ለእኔ ፍላጎቶች ትኩረት ይሰጣል።				
39	ስራየን የሚመለከቱ ዉሳኔዎች ሲተላለፉ የሚመለከተዉ የስራ ሃላፊ እዉነተኝነትን በተላበሰ መልኩ ያሳዉቀኛል።				

40	ስራየን የሚመለከቱ ውሳኔዎች ሲተላለፉ የሚመለከተዉ የስራ ሃላፊ ስለመብቶች ይጨነቃል።				
41	ስራየን የሚመለከቱ ዉሳኔዎችን ታሳቢ በማድረግ የሚመለከተዉ የስራ ሃላፊ የዉሳኔዎቹን እንደምታ አስመልክቶ ከኔ ጋር ዉይይት ያደርጋል።				
42	የሚመለከተዉ የስራ ሃላፊ ስራየን የሚመለከቱ ዉሳኔዎች ላይ በቂ ምክንያት ይሰጠኛል።				
43	ስራየን የሚመለከቱ ዉሳኔዎች ሲተላለፉ የሚመለከተዉ የስራ ሃላፊ ትርጉም ያለዉ ማብራሪያ ይሰጠኛል።				
44	የሚመለከተዉ የስራ ሃላፊ ማንኛዉንም ስራየን የሚመለከቱ ዉሳኔዎችን አስመልክቶ በጣም ግልፅ የሆነ ማብራሪያ ያደርግልኛል።				
ከመደበኛ ስራ ዉጭ የሆኑ ተግባራት	1	2	3	4	5
45	በስራ ላይ ያልተገኙ ሌሎች ሰዎችን እረዳቸዋለሁ።				
46	የስራ ጫና ያለባቸዉን ሌሎች ሰዎች እረዳቸዋለሁ።				
47	አዳዲስ ሰራተኞችን በማስተዋወቅ ረገድ አስፈላጊ ባይሆን እንኳን እረዳቸዋለሁ።				
48	ከስራ ጋር የተያያዘ ችግር ያለባቸዉን ሰዎች በራሴ መልካም ፈቃደኝነት እረዳቸዋለሁ።				
49	የእኔ እርዳታ የሚያስፈልጋቸዉን ሌሎች ሰዎች ለመርዳት ሁልጊዜ ዝግጁ ነኝ።				
50	ለእኔ በስራ ላይ መገኘት ከምንም ነገር በላይ ነዉ።				

51	ትርፍ የዕረፍት ጊዜ አልወስድም።					
52	ማንም ተመልካች ባይኖር እንኳን ለመስሪያ ቤቴን ህጎችና ደንቦች ተገዥ ነኝ።					
53	እኔ በጣም ጥንቁቅ ከሆኑ ሰራተኞ አንዱ ነኝ።					
54	ለሚከፈለኝ ተገቢ ክፍያ ተገቢዉን ስራ መስራት እንደምችል አምናለሁ።					
55	አብዛኛዉን ጊዜየን የማባክነዉ በጥቃቅን ነገሮች በማማረር ነዉ።					
56	ከጥቃቅን ነገሮች ተራራ አሳክሎ የማቅረብ ልምድ አለኝ።					
57	በአብዛኛዉ ጊዜ ከመልካም ነገሮች ይልቅ በስህተቶች ላይ ማተኮር ይቀናኛል።					
58	መስሪያ ቤቴ በሚያከናዉናቸዉ ነገሮች ላይ ሁልጊዜ ስሞተት እፈልጋለሁ።					
59	እኔ ሁልጊዜ ትኩረት ለመሳብ ስል ነገሮችን ማማረርና አጥብቄ መቃወም የምፈልግ ሰዉ ነኝ።					
60	ከሌሎች ሰራተኞች ጋር የሚፈጠሩ ችግሮችን ለመከላከል የሚያችሉ ርምጃዎችን እወስዳለሁ።					
61	የእኔ ባህሪይ ምን ያህል የሌሎች ሰዎችን ስራ ሊያዉክ እንደሚችል በትኩረት እከታተላለሁ።					
62	የሌሎች ሰዎችን መብት አልጋፋም።					
63	በሰራተኞች ላይ ችግር ላለመፍጠር እሞክራለሁ።					
64	የእኔ ድርጊቶች በሌሎች የስራ ባልደረቦች ላይ የሚያሳድሩት ተዕዕኖ ያሳስበኛል።					

65	አስገዳጅ ያልሆኑ ነር ግን ጠቃሚነት ያላቸዉን ስብስባዎች እካፈላለሁ።					
66	የመስሪያ ቤቴን ምስል የሚያጎሉ ነገር ግን ሃላፊነት የማያስከትሉ ተግባራትን አከናዉናለሁ።					
67	በመስሪያ ቤቴ ዉስጥ ወቅቱን የጠበቀ ለዉጥ አካል ነኝ።					
68	በመስሪያ ቤቴ ዉስጥ የሚተላለፉ ማስታወቂያዎችን፣ ማስታወሻዎችን እና የመሳሰሉትን በማንበብ አብሬ እንዛለሁ።					

Appendix-2- Rating Scale for Expert Judges

Addis Ababa University

College of Education and Behavioral Studies

School of Psychology

To Expert Judges

I. General Information

The study instruments that are to be tested for a pilot purpose are provided below to inter-rate accorded with the reliability significance of items in between the variables they are intended to measure. In this regard, you are sincerely requested to give your judgments on each and every items whether there are cases less from the minimal standards of the items in their measurement patterns. Hence the major help from your administration of items is inevitably very important input to the facilitation of this study with standardized expectations.

Moreover, in give you brief facts about the study, the following points are the prime concerns:

⇒   The major objective of the study is to examine Ethiopian public service employees' Organizational identification (OID), Job involvement (JI), Perceived organizational justice (OJ) as predictors of Organizational citizenship behavior (OCB) at a Federal level.

⇒   The Socio- demographic variables are part of the predictor variables and confounding ones to compare other independent variables with an outcome variable as well.

⇒   The instruments to be tested for this part are adapted from internationally recognized researchers in the area with reputation and constant reliability of the scales empirically.

⇒   The conceptualization of the instruments are depending on the factors that are discussed in the literature of the current study (there are different but technically mutual instruments to measure the study variables other than the selected version of measurements in varieties of contexts).

II   Expected Responses from Raters

Dear judges, you are asked to give authentic answers on the basis of two area mentioned below:

A.   Are these instruments (items) really measures what they are intended to measure?

B.   How ample is you perceive the strength of the instruments (items) to measure the specific variables in a continuum?

III - Description of Variables

1.   **Organizational Identification-** According to Meal & Ashforth (1991) Organizational identification is defined as a perceived oneness with an organization and the experience of the organization's successes and failures as one's own (*p.*103). This construct has cognitive and affective components   that are measured with six- items rated on point Likert scale and it is developed by Meal & Asforth (1991). The original reliability of this scale is 0.79.

2. Job Involvement- is a generalized cognitive state of psychological identification with the individual's cognition about his or her identification with work. (Kanugo , 1982, *p.* 131). The scale is composed of ten items measuring with Likert scale. The original reliability of this scale is 0.82.

3. Organizational Justice- is encompass the employees determination of wheter they have been treated fairly in their jobs and the influence that is brought by this determinations in the work-related variables.(Moorman, 1991).Organizational justice has three main dimensions: namely Distributive, Procedural and Interactional justice. For the purpose of this study, **Distributive justice** items are adapted from Price and Mueller (1986) with a six items, considering the amount of justice for allocation of organizational resources as a result of seeing employee responsibilities, education, experiences, and performance (Bez, 2010 p. 98). With regard to the second dimension, **Procedural justice** is measuring by Sweeney & McFarlan's (1997) scale with thirteen items, in terms of degree of employees' perception regarding whether their thoughts and needs are considered through making job decisions.(Bez, 2010 p. 98).Lastly, **Interactional justice** is measured by using Niehoff and Moorman' s (1993) 9-item scale, the major concern of employees' perception regarding whether their thoughts and needs are considered through making job decisions.(Bez, 2010 p. 98). The reliability coefficient of distributive justice is .74 -.98; Procedural justice is .84 -.85 and interactional justice is .92 - .98.

4. Organizational Citizenship Behavior- According to, (Organ, 1988) is an extra-role behavior that is discretionary and not explicitly related to the formal reward system of an organization but is conducive to its effective functioning. This construct has five dimensions: Namely

A. Altruism-These are actions that constructively contributes to help other persons in day to day work problem by instructing those individuals who are new to the organization in different situations. (Organ, 1988).Original reliability of this dimension is .67 - .89

B. Conscientiousness- it represents the awareness and performances of individuals in organizational contexts that are beyond the least possible necessities. (Organ, 1988).Original reliability of this dimension is .79

C. Sportsmanship- is the ability of individuals to show citizen-like posture in relationships with others by tolerating the inconveniences that are foreseeable and the capability of peoples to accept burdens of work without complaints and whims.(Organ, 1988). The original reliability of this dimension is .76 - .89

D. Courtesy- it is focused on the attainment in showing considerable gestures for others to prevent problems and contacting (keep in touch) with people to reduce actions that have negative consequences to people.(Organ, 1988).The original reliability of this dimension is .69-.86

E. Civic virtue-it is directed on the actual and active political participations of employees in the internal organizational context that could consists of expressing one's opinion and carefully reading the sending & received mails, be present in meetings, well-informed to organizational issues at large.(Organ, 1988).The original reliability of this dimension is .66-.99

The scale used to measure this construct is based on, Podsakoff et al.'s (1990) which is based on 24 items that is based on Likert scale formulation.

N.B- R-**in bracket means reversely coded items.**

Rater's Sex-----------------------------------

Educational Qualification-----------------

Job Qualification-----------------------------   use "X" for your selected answers

No	Organizational Identification Scale (Meal & Asforth ,1991)	Are these instruments (items) really measures what they are intended to measure?		How ample is you perceive the strength of the instruments (items) to measure the specific variables in a continuum?				
		Yes	No	Very Weak	Sl ight ly wea k	Weak	S tro ng	V ery stro ng
		1	2	1	2	3	4	5
1	When someone criticizes my organization, I feels like a personal insult.							
2	I am very interested in what others think about my organization.							
3	When I talk about my organization, I usually say we rather that they.							
4	This organizations success is my success							
5	When someone praise this organization, it feels like a personal compliment.							

6	If a story in a media criticized my organization, I would feel embarrassed.							

Job Involvement Scale
(Kanungo, 1982)

7	The most important things that happen to me involve my job.							
8	To me, my job is only a small part of who I am.(R)							
9	I am very much involved personally in my job.							
10	I live, eat and breathe my job.							
11	Most of my interests are centered around my job.							
12	I have very strong ties with my present job which would be very difficult to break.							
13	Usually I feel detached from my job.(R)							
14	Most of my personal life goals are job-oriented.							
15	I consider my job to be very central to my life.							
16	I like to be really involved in my job most of the time.							

Organizational justice Scale
Distributive justice
(Price & Mueller (1986)

17	When considering the responsibilities that I have, I am fairly rewarded.							
18	When taking into account the amount of education and training that I have, I am fairly rewarded.							
19	When in view of the amount of experience that I have, I am fairly rewarded.							

20	When considering the amount of effort that I put forth, I am fairly rewarded.							
21	When considering the work that I have done well, I am fairly rewarded.							
22	When considering the stresses and strains of my job, I am fairly rewarded.							
Procedural justice (Sweeney& McFarlin's 1997)								
23	I am not sure what determines how I can get a promotion in this organization.(R)							
24	I am told promptly when there's a change in policy, rules, or regulations that affects me.							
25	It's not really possible to change things around me.(R)							
26	There are adequate procedures to get my performance rating reconsidered if necessary.							
27	I understand the performance appraisal system being used in this organization.							
28	When changes are made in this organization, the employees usually lose out in the end. (R)							
29	Affirmative action policies have helped advance the employment opportunities in this organization.							
30	In general, disciplinary actions taken in this organization are fair and justified.							
31	I am not afraid to "blow the whistle" on things I find wrong with my organization.							

32	If I were subject to an involuntary personnel action, I believe my agency would adequately inform me of grievance and appeal rights.							
33	I am aware of the specific steps I must take to have a personnel action taken against mere considered.							
34	The procedures used to evaluate my performance have been fair and objective.							
35	In the past, I have been aware of what standards have been used to evaluate my performance.							
Interactional justice (Niehoff & Moorman, 1993)								
36	When decisions are made about my job, the general manager treats me with kindness and consideration.							
37	When decisions are made about my job, the general manager treats me with respect and dignity.							
38	When decisions are made about my job, the general manager is sensitive to my personal needs.							
39	When decisions are made about my job, the general manager deals with me in a truthful manner.							
40	When decisions are made about my job, the general manager shows concern for my rights as an employee.							

41	Concerning decisions about my job, the general manager discusses the implications of the decisions with me.							
42	The general manager offers adequate justification for decisions made about my job.							
43	When making decisions about my job, the general manager offers an explanation that makes sense to me.							
44	My general manager explains very clearly any decisions made about my job.							
Organizational citizenship behavior (Podsakoff et al.1990),Altruism								
45	I help others who have been absent.							
46	I help others who have heavy workloads.							
47	I help orient new people even though it is not required.							
48	I willingly help others who have work-related problems.							
49	I am always ready to lend a helping hand to those around me.							
Conscientiousness								
50	Attendance at work is above the norm for me.							
51	I do not take extra breaks.							
52	I obey company rules and regulations even when no one is watching.							
53	I'm one of most conscientious employees.							
54	I believe in giving an honest day's work for an honest day's pay.							

	Sportsmanship								
55	I consume a lot of time complaining about trivial matters. (R)								
56	I tend to make "mountains out of molehills". (R)								
57	I always focus on what's wrong rather than the positive side. (R)								
58	I always find fault with what the organization is doing. (R)								
59	I am the classic "squeaky wheel" that always needs greasing. (R)								
	Courtesy								
60	I take steps to try to prevent problems with other workers.								
61	I am mindful of how my behavior affects other people's job.								
62	I do not abuse the rights of others.								
63	I try to avoid creating problems for workers.								
64	I consider the impact of my actions on coworkers.								
	Civic virtue								
65	I attend meetings that are not mandatory, but are considered.								
66	I attend functions that are not required, but help the company image.								
67	I keep abreast of changes in the organization.								
68	I read and keep up with organizational announcements, memos, and so on.								

Appendix-3-Results of Descriptive Statistics Based on Socio-Demographic Characteristics of Participants

Gender		N	Mean	Std. Deviation	Std. Error
Overall OCB	Male	94	93.9594	11.79403	1.21646
	Female	108	93.9255	12.24753	1.17852
	Total	202	93.9413	12.00880	.84494
Altruism	Male	94	19.6983	3.29791	.34015
	Female	108	20.0397	3.71020	.35701
	Total	202	19.8808	3.51985	.24766
Conscientiousness	Male	94	20.1831	3.34711	.34523
	Female	108	20.2394	3.62880	.34918
	Total	202	20.2132	3.49203	.24570
Sportsmanship	Male	94	10.1041	3.94727	.40713
	Female	108	9.5106	4.17415	.40166
	Total	202	9.7868	4.07092	.28643
Courtesy	Male	94	19.2980	4.01831	.41446
	Female	108	18.7504	4.23853	.40785
	Total	202	19.0052	4.13635	.29103
Civic virtue	Male	94	14.7180	3.18365	.32837
	Female	108	14.9304	3.15596	.30368
	Total	202	14.8316	3.16276	.22253

Age groups		N	Mean	Std. Deviation	Std. Error
Overall OCB	18-29	49	94.9874	10.30226	1.47175
	30-40	92	91.8128	13.99424	1.45900
	41-50	43	96.1717	9.95291	1.51780
	>=51	18	96.6442	8.02287	1.89101
	Total	202	93.9413	12.00880	.84494
Altruism	18-29	49	20.4344	2.75696	.39385
	30-40	92	19.1061	4.15961	.43367
	41-50	43	20.6716	2.74129	.41804
	>=51	18	20.4444	2.79121	.65789
	Total	202	19.8808	3.51985	.24766

Conscientiousness	18-29	49	19.8950	2.45646	.35092
	30-40	92	19.7414	4.16407	.43413
	41-50	43	21.2093	3.06717	.46774
	>=51	18	21.1111	2.49444	.58794
	Total	202	20.2132	3.49203	.24570
Sportsmanship	18-29	49	10.2201	4.26388	.60913
	30-40	92	10.0303	4.17602	.43538
	41-50	43	9.1944	4.07732	.62179
	>=51	18	8.7778	2.71284	.63942
	Total	202	9.7868	4.07092	.28643
Courtesy	18-29	49	19.5308	4.57847	.65407
	30-40	92	18.3047	4.19513	.43737
	41-50	43	19.6283	3.27337	.49918
	>=51	18	19.6667	4.18681	.98684
	Total	202	19.0052	4.13635	.29103
Civic virtue	18-29	49	14.9693	3.45519	.49360
	30-40	92	14.4474	3.18659	.33222
	41-50	43	15.4340	3.17339	.48394
	>=51	18	14.9813	1.87946	.44299
	Total	202	14.8316	3.16276	.22253

Work Experience		N	Mean	Std. Deviation	Std. Error
Overall OCB	0-5	36	92.2388	12.37903	2.06317
	6-10	54	92.3699	13.96419	1.90029
	11-15	35	91.8854	13.01662	2.20021
	16-20	14	97.7424	7.86936	2.10318
	21-25	16	96.3497	10.44268	2.61067
	26-30	21	97.3044	11.18664	2.44112
	>31	26	96.0843	7.86439	1.54233
	Total	202	93.9413	12.00880	.84494
Altruism	0-5	36	19.8578	3.44046	.57341
	6-10	54	19.2504	3.67479	.50008
	11-15	35	19.2000	4.58129	.77438
	16-20	14	20.5714	2.73761	.73166
	21-25	16	21.0000	2.52982	.63246

	26-30	21	20.4172	3.07712	.67148
	>31	26	20.6447	2.67000	.52363
	Total	202	19.8808	3.51985	.24766
Conscientiousness	0-5	36	19.2281	3.66683	.61114
	6-10	54	20.0528	3.73669	.50850
	11-15	35	20.1143	4.15700	.70266
	16-20	14	20.3571	3.27243	.87459
	21-25	16	20.8125	2.56174	.64043
	26-30	21	21.2381	3.16077	.68974
	>31	26	20.7692	2.38843	.46841
	Total	202	20.2132	3.49203	.24570
Sportsmanship	0-5	36	10.8056	4.16667	.69444
	6-10	54	10.1217	4.56874	.62173
	11-15	35	9.4286	3.44952	.58307
	16-20	14	9.3419	4.64909	1.24252
	21-25	16	8.9375	4.46421	1.11605
	26-30	21	9.4184	4.15297	.90625
	>31	26	9.2226	2.92801	.57423
	Total	202	9.7868	4.07092	.28643
Courtesy	0-5	36	19.1390	4.40229	.73371
	6-10	54	18.1300	4.70674	.64051
	11-15	35	18.3432	4.35856	.73673
	16-20	14	20.0007	1.92112	.51344
	21-25	16	20.1253	3.84481	.96120
	26-30	21	20.0476	3.62596	.79125
	>31	26	19.4617	3.39680	.66617
	Total	202	19.0052	4.13635	.29103
Civic virtue	0-5	36	14.8795	3.75513	.62585
	6-10	54	14.7129	3.10396	.42240
	11-15	35	13.9236	3.54202	.59871
	16-20	14	16.2737	2.24151	.59907
	21-25	16	14.5520	3.50064	.87516
	26-30	21	15.9524	2.80136	.61131
	>31	26	14.7243	1.86603	.36596
	Total	202	14.8316	3.16276	.22253

Educational Status		N	Mean	Std. Deviation	Std. Error
Overall OCB	High School & Below	40	94.6048	13.98033	2.21048
	Vocational& Diploma	63	91.2757	13.34889	1.68180
	Under graduate	72	96.2942	9.29215	1.09509
	Post Graduate	27	92.9034	11.25347	2.16573
	Total	202	93.9413	12.00880	.84494
Altruism	High School & Below	40	19.7940	4.24364	.67098
	Vocational& Diploma	63	19.6432	4.04020	.50902
	Under graduate	72	20.3423	2.40483	.28341
	Post Graduate	27	19.3333	3.60555	.69389
	Total	202	19.8808	3.51985	.24766
Conscientiousness	High School & Below	40	19.7000	4.49615	.71090
	Vocational& Diploma	63	19.4705	3.60213	.45383
	Under graduate	72	21.1031	2.74624	.32365
	Post Graduate	27	20.3333	2.90887	.55981
	Total	202	20.2132	3.49203	.24570
Sportsmanship	High School & Below	40	9.6000	4.12497	.65222
	Vocational& Diploma	63	10.1134	4.04684	.50985
	Under graduate	72	9.2748	4.01087	.47269
	Post Graduate	27	10.6667	4.21536	.81125
	Total	202	9.7868	4.07092	.28643
Courtesy	High School & Below	40	19.2751	4.46632	.70619
	Vocational& Diploma	63	18.0161	4.62290	.58243
	Under graduate	72	19.6949	3.43395	.40470
	Post Graduate	27	19.0743	3.92159	.75471
	Total	202	19.0052	4.13635	.29103
Civic virtue	High School & Below	40	15.0666	3.35460	.53041
	Vocational& Diploma	63	14.2723	3.76269	.47405
	Under graduate	72	15.1458	2.59348	.30564
	Post Graduate	27	14.9505	2.68178	.51611
	Total	202	14.8316	3.16276	.22253

Monthly Income		N	Mean	Std. Deviation	Std. Error
Overall OCB	500-1500 Birr	33	92.1753	13.99484	2.43619
	1501-2500 Birr	25	93.9838	9.73840	1.94768
	2501-3500 Birr	22	92.7543	9.02099	1.92328
	3501-4500 Birr	39	92.4097	14.20505	2.27463
	4501-5500	21	95.3141	13.59011	2.96560
	5501-6500	15	96.5992	9.22289	2.38134
	>6501	47	95.5233	11.12481	1.62272
	Total	202	93.9413	12.00880	.84494
Altruism	500-1500 Birr	33	20.5382	3.29046	.57280
	1501-2500 Birr	25	18.6000	3.76386	.75277
	2501-3500 Birr	22	19.4491	3.56797	.76069
	3501-4500 Birr	39	19.9878	4.34696	.69607
	4501-5500	21	19.8038	3.14011	.68523
	5501-6500	15	20.9254	2.05581	.53081
	>6501	47	19.9149	3.24928	.47396
	Total	202	19.8808	3.51985	.24766
Conscientiousness	500-1500 Birr	33	20.0368	3.70389	.64476
	1501-2500 Birr	25	19.4800	3.56043	.71209
	2501-3500 Birr	22	19.1364	3.60285	.76813
	3501-4500 Birr	39	20.0420	4.12651	.66077
	4501-5500	21	20.3333	3.55434	.77562
	5501-6500	15	21.9475	2.27017	.58616
	>6501	47	20.7660	2.80692	.40943
	Total	202	20.2132	3.49203	.24570
Sportsmanship	500-1500 Birr	33	11.3875	4.48789	.78124
	1501-2500 Birr	25	8.3515	2.95173	.59035
	2501-3500 Birr	22	10.5455	3.41882	.72889
	3501-4500 Birr	39	9.5843	4.69408	.75165
	4501-5500	21	8.6565	4.47293	.97607
	5501-6500	15	9.5333	2.89992	.74876
	>6501	47	9.8253	3.89707	.56845
	Total	202	9.7868	4.07092	.28643
Courtesy	500-1500 Birr	33	18.5762	5.19637	.90457
	1501-2500 Birr	25	18.9200	3.93616	.78723
	2501-3500 Birr	22	18.3187	3.31510	.70678
	3501-4500 Birr	39	18.6669	4.94888	.79246

	4501-5500	21	19.4762	4.35453	.95024
	5501-6500	15	19.2014	3.64879	.94211
	>6501	47	19.6809	3.05106	.44504
	Total	202	19.0052	4.13635	.29103
Civic virtue	500-1500 Birr	33	14.6868	4.56488	.79464
	1501-2500 Birr	25	15.0733	2.27206	.45441
	2501-3500 Birr	22	14.5000	2.75595	.58757
	3501-4500 Birr	39	13.9741	3.35654	.53748
	4501-5500	21	15.1429	3.27545	.71476
	5501-6500	15	15.7109	2.38262	.61519
	>6501	47	15.2517	2.48058	.36183
	Total	202	14.8316	3.16276	.22253

Appendix-4-Normality Test Results

Gender

Descriptives

	Gender			Statistic	Std. Error
Overall OCB	Male	Mean		93.9594	1.21646
		95% Confidence Interval for Mean	Lower Bound	91.5437	
			Upper Bound	96.3750	
		5% Trimmed Mean		94.6558	
		Median		93.7977	
		Variance		139.099	
		Std. Deviation		11.79403	
		Minimum		49.00	
		Maximum		116.00	
		Range		67.00	
		Interquartile Range		14.25	
		Skewness		-1.133	.249
		Kurtosis		3.031	.493
	Female	Mean		93.9255	1.17852
		95% Confidence Interval for Mean	Lower Bound	91.5892	
			Upper Bound	96.2618	
		5% Trimmed Mean		94.6888	
		Median		93.7977	
		Variance		150.002	
		Std. Deviation		12.24753	
		Minimum		44.00	
		Maximum		115.00	
		Range		71.00	
		Interquartile Range		13.50	
		Skewness		-1.187	.233
		Kurtosis		2.837	.461

Extreme Values

	Gender			Case Number	Value
Overall OCB	Male	Highest	1	184	116.00
			2	185	114.00
			3	186	112.00
			4	196	112.00
			5	160	111.00[a]
		Lowest	1	162	49.00
			2	169	50.00
			3	201	64.00
			4	167	75.00
			5	147	78.00[b]
	Female	Highest	1	27	115.00
			2	9	114.00
			3	25	113.00
			4	99	112.00
			5	15	111.00[a]
		Lowest	1	45	44.00
			2	71	50.00
			3	92	64.00
			4	108	72.00
			5	107	72.00[c]

a. Only a partial list of cases with the value 111.00 are shown in the table of upper extremes.

b. Only a partial list of cases with the value 78.00 are shown in the table of lower extremes.

c. Only a partial list of cases with the value 72.00 are shown in the table of lower extremes.

Tests of Normality

		Kolmogorov-Smirnov[a]			Shapiro-Wilk		
	Gender	Statistic	df	Sig.	Statistic	df	Sig.
Overall OCB	Male	.103	94	.015	.928	94	.000
	Female	.163	108	.000	.923	108	.000

a. Lilliefors Significance Correction

Overall OCB
Normal Q-Q Plots

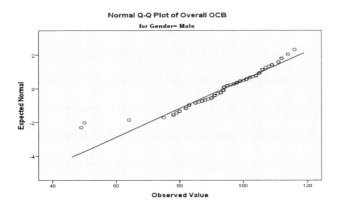

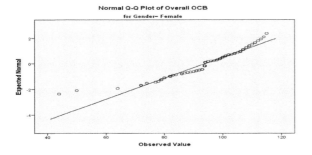

Detrended Normal Q-Q Plots

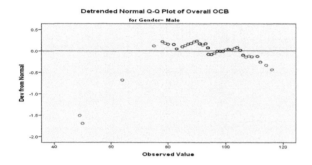

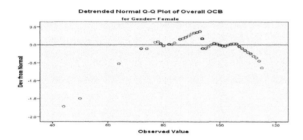

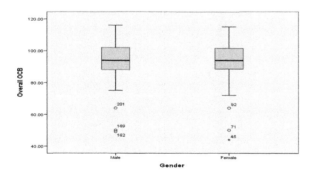

Descriptives

	Age			Statistic	Std. Error
Overall OCB	18-29	Mean		94.9874	1.47175
		95% Confidence Interval for Mean	Lower Bound	92.0282	
			Upper Bound	97.9465	
		5% Trimmed Mean		95.1730	
		Median		93.7977	
		Variance		106.137	
		Std. Deviation		10.30226	
		Minimum		72.00	
		Maximum		116.00	
		Range		44.00	
		Interquartile Range		12.50	
		Skewness		-.261	.340
		Kurtosis		.011	.668
	30-40	Mean		91.8128	1.45900
		95% Confidence Interval for Mean	Lower Bound	88.9146	
			Upper Bound	94.7109	
		5% Trimmed Mean		92.9804	
		Median		93.7977	
		Variance		195.839	
		Std. Deviation		13.99424	
		Minimum		44.00	
		Maximum		114.00	
		Range		70.00	
		Interquartile Range		14.50	
		Skewness		-1.290	.251
		Kurtosis		2.415	.498
	41-50	Mean		96.1717	1.51780
		95% Confidence Interval for Mean	Lower Bound	93.1086	
			Upper Bound	99.2347	
		5% Trimmed Mean		96.1726	
		Median		94.0000	
		Variance		99.060	
		Std. Deviation		9.95291	
		Minimum		78.00	

		Maximum		115.00	
		Range		37.00	
		Interquartile Range		13.00	
		Skewness		-.184	.361
		Kurtosis		-.678	.709
	>=51	Mean		96.6442	1.89101
		95% Confidence Interval for	Lower Bound	92.6545	
		Mean	Upper Bound	100.6339	
		5% Trimmed Mean		96.7158	
		Median		97.5000	
		Variance		64.367	
		Std. Deviation		8.02287	
		Minimum		83.00	
		Maximum		109.00	
		Range		26.00	
		Interquartile Range		13.50	
		Skewness		-.244	.536
		Kurtosis		-1.014	1.038

Extreme Values

	Age			Case Number	Value
Overall OCB	18-29	Highest	1	184	116.00
			2	185	114.00
			3	160	111.00
			4	86	109.00
			5	48	108.00[a]
		Lowest	1	108	72.00
			2	107	72.00
			3	59	74.00
			4	53	77.00
			5	154	82.00[b]
	30-40	Highest	1	9	114.00
			2	99	112.00
			3	186	112.00

		4	196	112.00
		5	166	111.00
	Lowest	1	45	44.00
		2	162	49.00
		3	169	50.00
		4	71	50.00
		5	201	64.00^c
41-50	Highest	1	27	115.00
		2	25	113.00
		3	15	111.00
		4	17	111.00
		5	125	109.00
	Lowest	1	132	78.00
		2	115	79.00
		3	26	79.00
		4	16	79.00
		5	114	82.00^b
>=51	Highest	1	127	109.00
		2	122	107.00
		3	142	106.00
		4	31	104.00
		5	42	104.00
	Lowest	1	130	83.00
		2	128	85.00
		3	38	86.00
		4	29	86.00
		5	133	92.00

a. Only a partial list of cases with the value 108.00 are shown in the table of upper extremes.

b. Only a partial list of cases with the value 82.00 are shown in the table of lower extremes.

c. Only a partial list of cases with the value 64.00 are shown in the table of lower extremes.

Tests of Normality

Age		Kolmogorov-Smirnov[a]			Shapiro-Wilk		
		Statistic	df	Sig.	Statistic	df	Sig.
Overall OCB	18-29	.117	49	.089	.971	49	.269
	30-40	.155	92	.000	.900	92	.000
	41-50	.150	43	.016	.954	43	.083
	>=51	.130	18	.200[*]	.950	18	.428

*. This is a lower bound of the true significance.

a. Lilliefors Significance Correction

Overall OCB

Normal Q-Q Plots

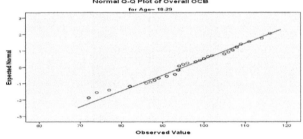

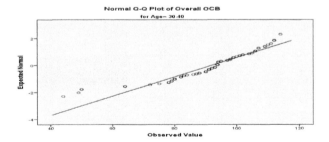

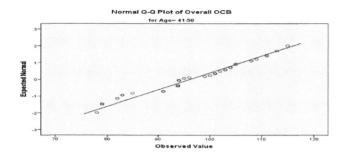

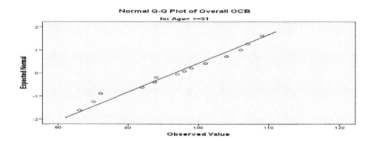

Detrended Normal Q-Q Plots

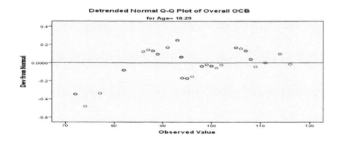

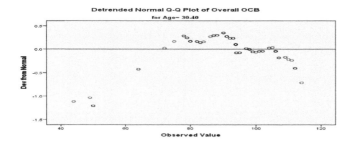

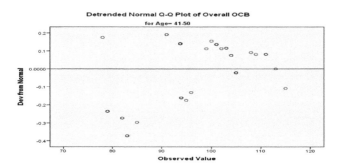

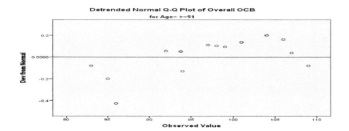

Boxplots

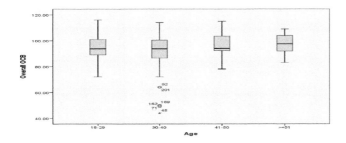

Experience

Descriptives

	Experience			Statistic	Std. Error
Overall OCB	0-5	Mean		92.2388	2.06317
		95% Confidence Interval for Mean	Lower Bound	88.0503	
			Upper Bound	96.4272	
		5% Trimmed Mean		93.2097	
		Median		93.8988	
		Variance		153.240	
		Std. Deviation		12.37903	
		Minimum		44.00	
		Maximum		111.00	
		Range		67.00	
		Interquartile Range		13.50	
		Skewness		-1.702	.393
		Kurtosis		5.392	.768
	6-10	Mean		92.3699	1.90029
		95% Confidence Interval for Mean	Lower Bound	88.5585	
			Upper Bound	96.1814	
		5% Trimmed Mean		93.5448	
		Median		93.7977	
		Variance		194.999	
		Std. Deviation		13.96419	
		Minimum		49.00	

	Maximum		116.00	
	Range		67.00	
	Interquartile Range		15.00	
	Skewness		-1.372	.325
	Kurtosis		3.065	.639
11-15	Mean		91.8854	2.20021
	95% Confidence Interval for Mean	Lower Bound	87.4140	
		Upper Bound	96.3567	
	5% Trimmed Mean		92.3171	
	Median		93.7977	
	Variance		169.432	
	Std. Deviation		13.01662	
	Minimum		64.00	
	Maximum		112.00	
	Range		48.00	
	Interquartile Range		21.00	
	Skewness		-.526	.398
	Kurtosis		-.317	.778
16-20	Mean		97.7424	2.10318
	95% Confidence Interval for Mean	Lower Bound	93.1987	
		Upper Bound	102.2860	
	5% Trimmed Mean		97.9915	
	Median		94.5000	
	Variance		61.927	
	Std. Deviation		7.86936	
	Minimum		82.00	
	Maximum		109.00	
	Range		27.00	
	Interquartile Range		12.40	
	Skewness		-.169	.597
	Kurtosis		-.528	1.154
21-25	Mean		96.3497	2.61067
	95% Confidence Interval for Mean	Lower Bound	90.7852	
		Upper Bound	101.9142	
	5% Trimmed Mean		96.3330	

		Median	95.0000	
		Variance	109.050	
		Std. Deviation	10.44268	
		Minimum	79.00	
		Maximum	114.00	
		Range	35.00	
		Interquartile Range	12.50	
		Skewness	.021	.564
		Kurtosis	-.407	1.091
26-30		Mean	97.3044	2.44112
	95% Confidence Interval for Mean	Lower Bound	92.2123	
		Upper Bound	102.3965	
		5% Trimmed Mean	97.3965	
		Median	100.0000	
		Variance	125.141	
		Std. Deviation	11.18664	
		Minimum	78.00	
		Maximum	115.00	
		Range	37.00	
		Interquartile Range	19.50	
		Skewness	-.259	.501
		Kurtosis	-1.043	.972
>31		Mean	96.0843	1.54233
	95% Confidence Interval for Mean	Lower Bound	92.9078	
		Upper Bound	99.2608	
		5% Trimmed Mean	96.2646	
		Median	94.0000	
		Variance	61.849	
		Std. Deviation	7.86439	
		Minimum	78.00	
		Maximum	110.00	
		Range	32.00	
		Interquartile Range	10.00	
		Skewness	-.221	.456
		Kurtosis	-.119	.887

Extreme Values

	Experience			Case Number	Value
Overall OCB	0-5	Highest	1	160	111.00
			2	48	108.00
			3	151	108.00
			4	149	105.00
			5	42	104.00
		Lowest	1	45	44.00
			2	59	74.00
			3	53	77.00
			4	147	78.00
			5	154	82.00[a]
	6-10	Highest	1	184	116.00
			2	185	114.00
			3	166	111.00
			4	86	109.00
			5	72	107.00[b]
		Lowest	1	162	49.00
			2	169	50.00
			3	71	50.00
			4	167	75.00
			5	178	80.00[c]
	11-15	Highest	1	99	112.00
			2	186	112.00
			3	196	112.00
			4	106	106.00
			5	187	106.00
		Lowest	1	201	64.00
			2	92	64.00
			3	108	72.00
			4	107	72.00
			5	95	72.00
	16-20	Highest	1	8	109.00
			2	6	108.00

		3	1	106.00
		4	7	106.00
		5	112	103.00
	Lowest	1	114	82.00
		2	110	90.00
		3	109	93.00
		4	5	93.80
		5	4	93.80[d]
21-25	Highest	1	9	114.00
		2	15	111.00
		3	17	111.00
		4	116	105.00
		5	14	100.00
	Lowest	1	115	79.00
		2	16	79.00
		3	117	85.00
		4	119	91.00
		5	11	92.00
26-30	Highest	1	27	115.00
		2	25	113.00
		3	125	109.00
		4	127	109.00
		5	122	107.00
	Lowest	1	24	78.00
		2	26	79.00
		3	30	82.00
		4	128	85.00
		5	29	86.00
>31	Highest	1	34	110.00
		2	35	109.00
		3	142	106.00
		4	146	105.00
		5	31	104.00[e]
	Lowest	1	132	78.00
		2	130	83.00

	3	38	86.00
	4	131	87.00
	5	143	91.00[f]

a. Only a partial list of cases with the value 82.00 are shown in the table of lower extremes.

b. Only a partial list of cases with the value 107.00 are shown in the table of upper extremes.

c. Only a partial list of cases with the value 80.00 are shown in the table of lower extremes.

d. Only a partial list of cases with the value 93.80 are shown in the table of lower extremes.

e. Only a partial list of cases with the value 104.00 are shown in the table of upper extremes.

f. Only a partial list of cases with the value 91.00 are shown in the table of lower extremes.

Tests of Normality

		Kolmogorov-Smirnov[a]			Shapiro-Wilk		
	Experience	Statistic	df	Sig.	Statistic	df	Sig.
Overall OCB	0-5	.136	36	.092	.881	36	.001
	6-10	.173	54	.000	.874	54	.000
	11-15	.163	35	.020	.943	35	.071
	16-20	.208	14	.104	.921	14	.231
	21-25	.117	16	.200*	.952	16	.522
	26-30	.119	21	.200*	.952	21	.376
	>31	.143	26	.183	.975	26	.757

*. This is a lower bound of the true significance.

a. Lilliefors Significance Correction

Overall OCB

Normal Q-Q Plots

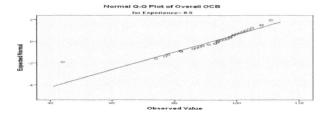

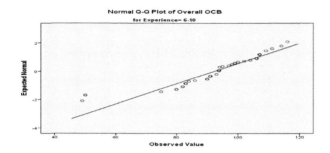

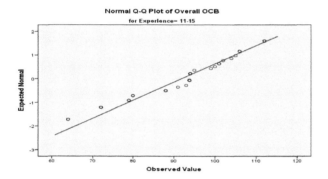

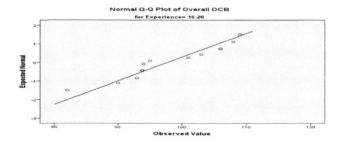

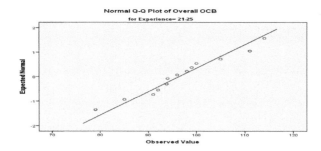

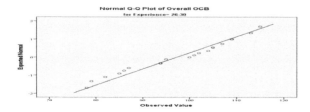

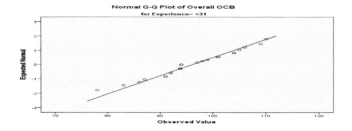

Detrended Normal Q-Q Plots

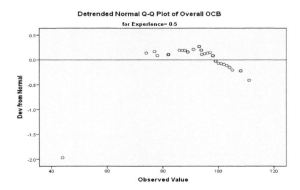

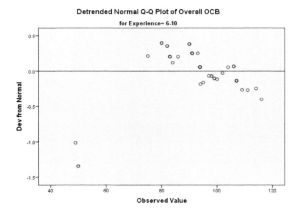

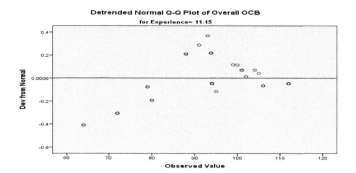

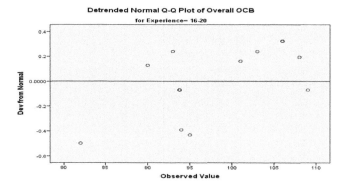

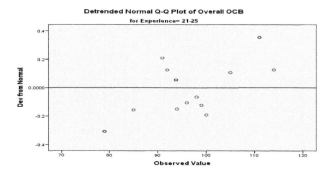

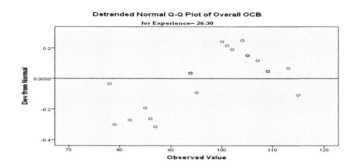

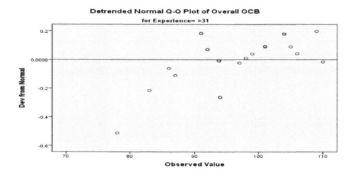

Boxplots

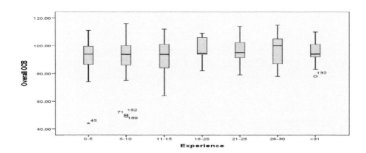

Education

Descriptives

	Education			Statistic	Std. Error
Overall OCB	Preparatory & Below	Mean		94.6048	2.21048
		95% Confidence Interval for Mean	Lower Bound	90.1336	
			Upper Bound	99.0759	
		5% Trimmed Mean		95.7275	
		Median		95.5000	
		Variance		195.450	
		Std. Deviation		13.98033	
		Minimum		44.00	
		Maximum		116.00	
		Range		72.00	
		Interquartile Range		16.75	
		Skewness		-1.340	.374
		Kurtosis		3.368	.733
	Vocational& Diploma	Mean		91.2757	1.68180
		95% Confidence Interval for Mean	Lower Bound	87.9138	

	Upper Bound		94.6376	
	5% Trimmed Mean		92.3875	
	Median		93.7977	
	Variance		178.193	
	Std. Deviation		13.34889	
	Minimum		49.00	
	Maximum		115.00	
	Range		66.00	
	Interquartile Range		13.00	
	Skewness		-1.346	.302
	Kurtosis		2.753	.595
Under graduate	Mean		96.2942	1.09509
	95% Confidence Interval for Mean	Lower Bound	94.1106	
		Upper Bound	98.4777	
	5% Trimmed Mean		96.5861	
	Median		95.0000	
	Variance		86.344	
	Std. Deviation		9.29215	
	Minimum		74.00	
	Maximum		112.00	
	Range		38.00	
	Interquartile Range		13.75	
	Skewness		-.365	.283
	Kurtosis		-.399	.559
Post Graduate	Mean		92.9034	2.16573
	95% Confidence Interval for Mean	Lower Bound	88.4517	
		Upper Bound	97.3552	
	5% Trimmed Mean		93.1643	
	Median		93.7977	
	Variance		126.641	
	Std. Deviation		11.25347	

Minimum	64.00	
Maximum	114.00	
Range	50.00	
Interquartile Range	18.00	
Skewness	-.286	.448
Kurtosis	.365	.872

Extreme Values

	Education			Case Number	Value
Overall OCB	Preparatory & Below	Highest	1	184	116.00
			2	9	114.00
			3	25	113.00
			4	186	112.00
			5	166	111.00
		Lowest	1	45	44.00
			2	92	64.00
			3	132	78.00
			4	94	79.00
			5	62	80.00
	Vocational& Diploma	Highest	1	27	115.00
			2	99	112.00
			3	86	109.00
			4	151	108.00
			5	88	107.00
		Lowest	1	162	49.00
			2	169	50.00
			3	71	50.00
			4	108	72.00
			5	107	72.00[a]
	Under graduate	Highest	1	196	112.00
			2	15	111.00
			3	160	111.00
			4	34	110.00
			5	35	109.00[b]

	Lowest	1	59	74.00
		2	167	75.00
		3	147	78.00
		4	105	79.00
		5	198	80.00ᶜ
Post Graduate	Highest	1	185	114.00
		2	17	111.00
		3	8	109.00
		4	7	106.00
		5	194	102.00
	Lowest	1	201	64.00
		2	16	79.00
		3	178	80.00
		4	154	82.00
		5	114	82.00

a. Only a partial list of cases with the value 72.00 are shown in the table of lower extremes.

b. Only a partial list of cases with the value 109.00 are shown in the table of upper extremes.

c. Only a partial list of cases with the value 80.00 are shown in the table of lower extremes.

Tests of Normality

	Education	Kolmogorov-Smirnov[a]			Shapiro-Wilk		
		Statistic	df	Sig.	Statistic	df	Sig.
Overall OCB	Preparatory & Below	.154	40	.018	.909	40	.003
	Vocational& Diploma	.155	63	.001	.888	63	.000
	Under graduate	.076	72	.200*	.966	72	.048
	Post Graduate	.091	27	.200*	.976	27	.759

*. This is a lower bound of the true significance.

a. Lilliefors Significance Correction

Overall OCB

Normal Q-Q Plots

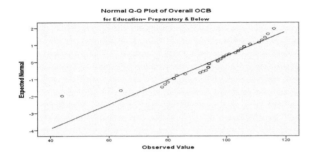

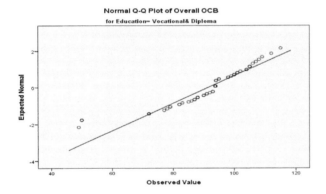

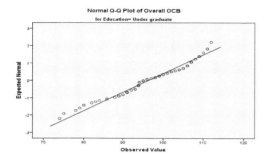

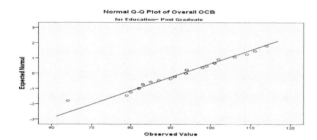

Detrended Normal Q-Q Plots

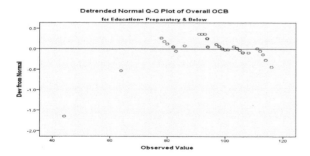

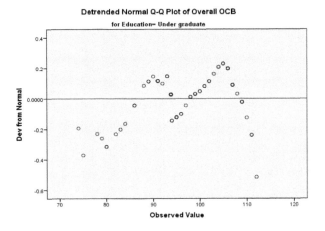

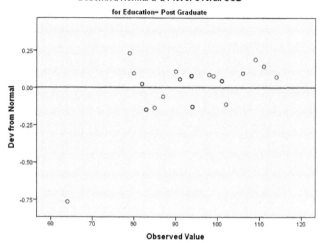

Detrended Normal Q-Q Plot of Overall OCB
for Education= Post Graduate

Boxplots

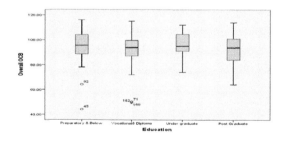

Income

Descriptives

	Income			Statistic	Std. Error
Overall OCB	500-1500 Birr	Mean		92.1753	2.43619
		95% Confidence Interval for Mean	Lower Bound	87.2130	
			Upper Bound	97.1377	
		5% Trimmed Mean		93.0770	
		Median		93.7977	
		Variance		195.855	
		Std. Deviation		13.99484	
		Minimum		49.00	
		Maximum		114.00	
		Range		65.00	
		Interquartile Range		17.00	
		Skewness		-1.129	.409
		Kurtosis		1.724	.798
	1501-2500 Birr	Mean		93.9838	1.94768
		95% Confidence Interval for Mean	Lower Bound	89.9640	
			Upper Bound	98.0036	
		5% Trimmed Mean		94.3820	
		Median		98.0000	
		Variance		94.836	
		Std. Deviation		9.73840	
		Minimum		72.00	
		Maximum		108.00	
		Range		36.00	
		Interquartile Range		13.50	
		Skewness		-.617	.464
		Kurtosis		-.451	.902
	2501-3500 Birr	Mean		92.7543	1.92328
		95% Confidence Interval for Mean	Lower Bound	88.7547	

		Upper Bound	96.7540	
	5% Trimmed Mean		92.4442	
	Median		93.0000	
	Variance		81.378	
	Std. Deviation		9.02099	
	Minimum		78.00	
	Maximum		113.00	
	Range		35.00	
	Interquartile Range		6.50	
	Skewness		.732	.491
	Kurtosis		.831	.953
3501-4500 Birr	Mean		92.4097	2.27463
	95% Confidence Interval for Mean	Lower Bound	87.8049	
		Upper Bound	97.0144	
	5% Trimmed Mean		93.7899	
	Median		93.7977	
	Variance		201.783	
	Std. Deviation		14.20505	
	Minimum		44.00	
	Maximum		115.00	
	Range		71.00	
	Interquartile Range		12.00	
	Skewness		-1.643	.378
	Kurtosis		4.071	.741
4501-5500	Mean		95.3141	2.96560
	95% Confidence Interval for Mean	Lower Bound	89.1279	
		Upper Bound	101.5002	
	5% Trimmed Mean		96.8384	
	Median		98.0000	
	Variance		184.691	
	Std. Deviation		13.59011	

	Minimum		50.00	
	Maximum		112.00	
	Range		62.00	
	Interquartile Range		14.50	
	Skewness		-1.914	.501
	Kurtosis		5.411	.972
5501-6500	Mean		96.5992	2.38134
	95% Confidence Interval for Mean	Lower Bound	91.4918	
		Upper Bound	101.7067	
	5% Trimmed Mean		96.2769	
	Median		94.0000	
	Variance		85.062	
	Std. Deviation		9.22289	
	Minimum		83.00	
	Maximum		116.00	
	Range		33.00	
	Interquartile Range		4.20	
	Skewness		.949	.580
	Kurtosis		.861	1.121
>6501	Mean		95.5233	1.62272
	95% Confidence Interval for Mean	Lower Bound	92.2569	
		Upper Bound	98.7897	
	5% Trimmed Mean		95.9361	
	Median		99.0000	
	Variance		123.761	
	Std. Deviation		11.12481	
	Minimum		64.00	
	Maximum		111.00	
	Range		47.00	
	Interquartile Range		19.00	
	Skewness		-.542	.347
	Kurtosis		-.290	.681

Extreme Values

	Income			Case Number	Value
Overall OCB	500-1500 Birr	Highest	1	9	114.00
			2	186	112.00
			3	48	108.00
			4	106	106.00
			5	93	105.00[a]
		Lowest	1	162	49.00
			2	92	64.00
			3	108	72.00
			4	107	72.00
			5	53	77.00
	1501-2500 Birr	Highest	1	151	108.00
			2	1	106.00
			3	187	106.00
			4	31	104.00
			5	188	104.00
		Lowest	1	95	72.00
			2	24	78.00
			3	94	79.00
			4	43	82.00
			5	130	83.00
	2501-3500 Birr	Highest	1	25	113.00
			2	99	112.00
			3	85	107.00
			4	152	98.00
			5	2	94.00[b]
		Lowest	1	132	78.00
			2	100	80.00
			3	154	82.00
			4	55	82.00
			5		
				56	86.00
	3501-4500 Birr	Highest	1	27	115.00

		2	166	111.00
		3	34	110.00
		4	86	109.00
		5	72	107.00
	Lowest	1	45	44.00
		2	71	50.00
		3	59	74.00
		4	167	75.00
		5	115	79.00[c]
4501-5500	Highest	1	196	112.00
		2	35	109.00
		3	88	107.00
		4	122	107.00
		5	74	106.00
	Lowest	1	169	50.00
		2	147	78.00
		3	117	85.00
		4	29	86.00
		5	183	91.00[d]
5501-6500	Highest	1	184	116.00
		2	185	114.00
		3	77	107.00
		4	118	98.00
		5	90	95.00[e]
	Lowest	1	172	83.00
		2	78	84.00
		3	123	93.80
		4	104	93.80
		5	79	93.80[f]
>6501	Highest	1	15	111.00
		2	17	111.00
		3	160	111.00
		4	8	109.00
		5	125	109.00[g]

Lowest	1		201	64.00
	2		105	79.00
	3		16	79.00
	4		198	80.00
	5		178	80.00

a. Only a partial list of cases with the value 105.00 are shown in the table of upper extremes.
b. Only a partial list of cases with the value 94.00 are shown in the table of upper extremes.
c. Only a partial list of cases with the value 79.00 are shown in the table of lower extremes.
d. Only a partial list of cases with the value 91.00 are shown in the table of lower extremes.
e. Only a partial list of cases with the value 95.00 are shown in the table of upper extremes.
f. Only a partial list of cases with the value 93.80 are shown in the table of lower extremes.
g. Only a partial list of cases with the value 109.00 are shown in the table of upper extremes.

Tests of Normality

	Income	Kolmogorov-Smirnov[a]			Shapiro-Wilk		
		Statistic	df	Sig.	Statistic	df	Sig.
Overall OCB	500-1500 Birr	.213	33	.001	.923	33	.022
	1501-2500 Birr	.180	25	.036	.944	25	.186
	2501-3500 Birr	.263	22	.000	.895	22	.024
	3501-4500 Birr	.209	39	.000	.853	39	.000
	4501-5500	.185	21	.059	.841	21	.003
	5501-6500	.302	15	.001	.821	15	.007
	>6501	.157	47	.005	.938	47	.015

a. Lilliefors Significance Correction

Overall OCB

Normal Q-Q Plots

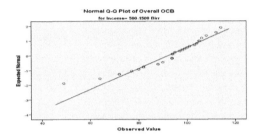

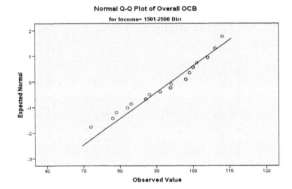

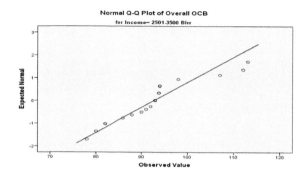

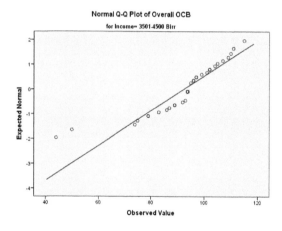

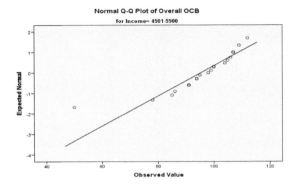

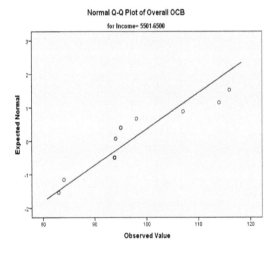

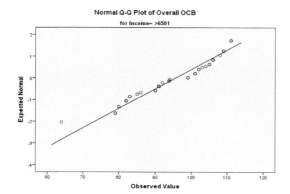

Detrended Normal Q-Q Plots

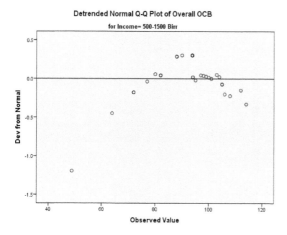

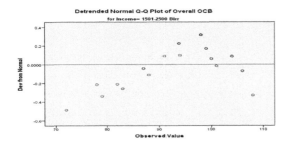

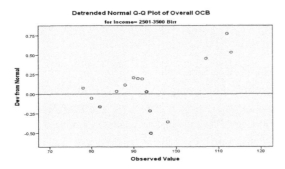

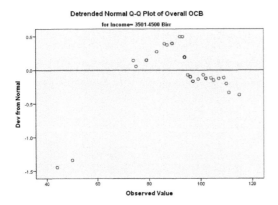

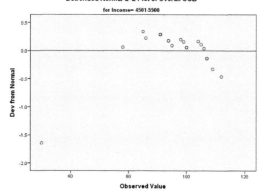

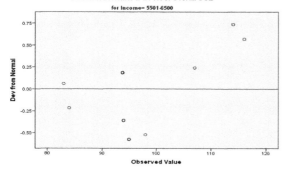

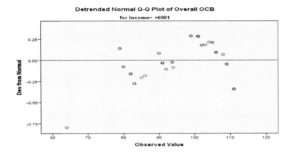

Boxplots

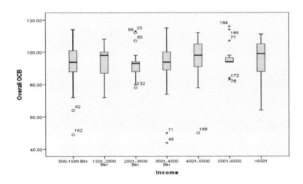

YOUR KNOWLEDGE HAS VALUE